26/2/20

Sometimes in Bath

Her Stories and History

Charles Nevin

Praise for previous books by Charles Nevin

Lancashire, Where Women Die of Love:

"An absolute joy... an admirable, engaging portrait. Nevin has a wonderful eye for observation."
Joanna Lumley

"The book that has amused me most in the last few months... full of lovely anecdotes and some rather good jokes"
Jeremy Paxman

Lost in the Wash With Other Things:

"This is a book of pure delight. Charles Nevin is a writer of wit, charm, and above all, humour."
Matthew Fort, writer and critic

"Very funny... strongly recommended."
Francis Wheen, journalist, author and broadcaster

First published in Great Britain in 2019 by
The Book Guild Ltd
9 Priory Business Park
Wistow Road, Kibworth
Leicestershire, LE8 0RX
Freephone: 0800 999 2982
www.bookguild.co.uk
Email: info@bookguild.co.uk
Twitter: @bookguild

Typeset in Minion Pro

Printed and bound in the UK by TJ International, Padstow, Cornwall

ISBN 978 1912881 826

British Library Cataloguing in Publication Data.
A catalogue record for this book is available from the British Library.

*For all who come to and from this
most enchanting and enchanted of cities*

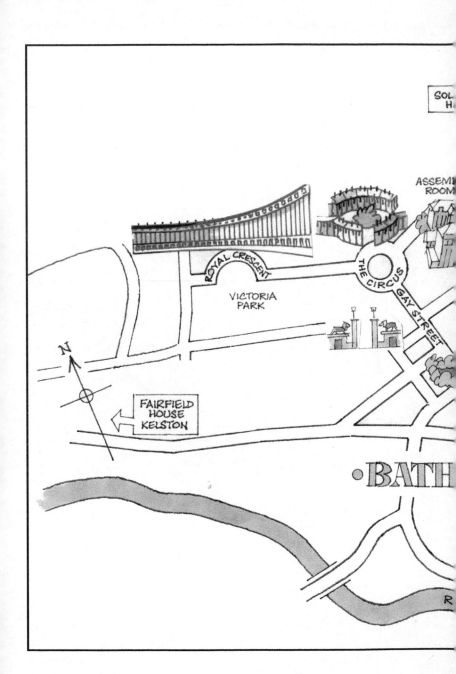

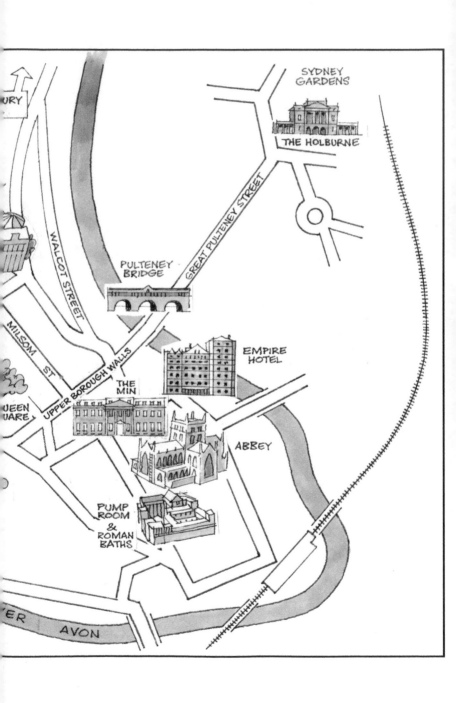

Contents

Bath, Oliver?

WELCOME TO BATH! IT IS THE MIDDLE OF THE eighteenth Century and we are down by the old Pump Room, where there is the usual commotion of chairs and crutches, passing gamesters, assorted rogues, ladies and gentlemen, unimpeachable and otherwise, old and young, fierce and fluttering, frowning and frowsy; where the air is full of chatter and the cries and wheedles of sellers of cures and trinkets, all set off by the clatter on the cobbles. That well-set, open-eyed young man is Tom Atkins; it is his first ever morning in Bath, and he has just stood on the foot of Dr William Oliver, esteemed physician and founder of the Royal Mineral Water Hospital, established for the halt and indigent.

Tom arrived from deepest Devon the night before, and is finding it considerably busier than South Zeal on a September day. Which partly explains his mishap with the doctor. He was pretty sure he'd trodden on something; this was confirmed by a yelp, a very loud yelp, more of an agonised scream, really. Tom put such a reaction

1

down to the softer, more refined ways of Bath gentlemen; apologising as much as he could, and mentioning that he'd had the odd cow tread on his foot from time to time, he helped the doctor to the nearest wall, all benches, nooks and niches being taken by the invalids and general loiterers, many of whom were concealing those smiles so often provoked by the misfortunes of others.

'Thank you, clumsy boy,' said the doctor, leaning and wincing. Of middle age and a generous figure, he had a large nose made to be offset by a wig, which was worn haphazardly. He was not a tidy man, nor a handsome one, and certainly not a thin one, but, as you might have deduced, there was a kindliness about him, even in such unpromising circumstances. 'Can you get my slipper off?' he asked, between deep sighs of the sort which gout sufferers will know too well. Tom, delighted to be of help, readily grasped the doctor's slipper, then yanked.

He didn't think the doctor could have yelped any louder than before, but he was wrong. Half of Bath turned round, surprised, quizzical, or just bored. 'Do you think you could be just a touch more gentle?' panted the doctor. 'I'm sure cows are more forgiving, and horses, and probably pigs, too, but my foot really is very sore.' I'm not certain you can speak in a wince, but the doctor was close. He had his arm on Tom's shoulder now, with his slipperless foot held out cautiously before him. 'Gout,' he said. 'Not much call for it in the country, I know, what with all the bucolic clean-living. It's an excruciating pain in the big toe, made even more excruciating by the sufferer's knowledge that he – and it always is a he – has no one and nothing to blame but his own excesses.'

No, he said, he didn't think this was the time or the place to go into what these excesses might be; he was rather late and could Tom get him a Sedan? It was lucky that the doctor was pointing at a small carriage without wheels standing nearby as otherwise Tom wouldn't have had a clue what he was talking about. South Zeal again. He went over to the carriage, observed the long parallel poles attached to the sides, and was working out how to pick it up when two men approached. They were wearing long, light-blue coats and large cocked hats bound with gold lace. One was quite tall, and the other was quite small. One's coat was a touch too large, the other's too small, as were their cocked hats.

'Yes?' said the smaller man. 'You after a lift?'

'That's very kind,' said Tom. 'But I'm all right on my own two feet. As a matter of fact, you might be interested to know that I've just walked here from South Zeal.'

'Amazing,' said the smaller man. The taller one said nothing.

'Your companion seems agitated,' said the smaller man.

Tom looked back; the doctor was indeed hopping up and down and waving at him.

'Sorry, yes, he wants a Sedan,' said Tom.

'Then you've come to the right place. We – my friend here Edgar and I – are such a said Sedan. In which direction is he desirous of travelling?'

'Does it matter?'

'Does it matter? Observe Edgar and my good self and our height differential. North from here is uphill, south downhill. If it's to be north, then, obviously, for maximum speed and comfort, I will go at the front, and Edgar will go at the back. If it's to be south, then *vice versa,* as the Roman gentlemen who lived here used to say at least twice a day, three if they were feeling perky. And then, of course, there's the northern surcharge.'

'Northern surcharge? What damned northern surcharge?' This was from the doctor, whose temper had not been improved by his slow hobble across.

'Ah, Doctor, I thought it was you, but I didn't think a medical man would be in such a sad state. Physician, heal thyself, and all that. The northern surcharge, an extra two pennies on the six, has just been introduced on account of journeys in that direction being harder work.'

'An extra two pennies?!' cried the doctor. 'That's a bit steep!'

'Exactly,' said Silas.

'But I want to go west, to my hospital!'

'Apologies, Doctor, but – and here I speak as a graduate of the Bath Sedan Chairmen Knowledge Appropriation Academy – your hospital is in fact north-north-west of here, which means that, most fortunately for you, your journey will attract only a penny surcharge. Isn't that so, Edgar?'

Edgar, who had remained expressionless throughout the exchange, spoke at last: 'It is, Silas.' He had a surprisingly high voice.

The doctor was getting ever more agitated: 'An extra penny!? But the hospital's only 400 yards at the most!'

'It'll seem longer with that limp, Doctor.'

This was the moment for an innocent and honest young man from Devon to stand up and be counted, and Tom did not fail. 'What? Only 400 yards? That's just the hop of a frog to a South Zeal man. Jump on my back, Sir, and we'll be there before you can say Silas and Edgar are a pair of platter-faced ninnycocks!'

Silas and Edgar thought this very funny. 'You're in Bath now, boy,' said Edgar. 'Things are managed with a little more decorum here than in some bumpkin village, wouldn't you say, Doctor?'

Dr Oliver was a man conscious of his status, but he was not a snob or a prig. He was a Cornishman by birth. When he was not suffering from gout, or being grave with one of his patients, he much enjoyed a laugh. Nor did he take himself as seriously as most of the rest of Bath, especially those sufferers present for the cure who tended to stand heavily on what was left of their dignity after drinking foul-tasting hot water and appearing semi-naked before their fellows. And his foot was very painful. Giving Silas, and Edgar, a look that wouldn't have disgraced a duchess encountering a posterior reverberation, he climbed on to Tom's back and put his arms round his neck.

Tom grasped the Doctor's legs and set off at a good lick. The Doctor, who found he was enjoying the stir his journey was causing, took one arm from Tom's neck at regular intervals and saluted passers-by, who, depending on status and inclination, were either cheering or jeering. Excitement became even more pronounced when, just as they were approaching the Mineral Hospital, the distinctive cream hat of Richard 'Beau' Nash, the promoter of Bath and arbiter of its social arrangements, was spotted approaching.

'Ah, Oliver,' said the Beau. 'Interesting rig you've got there. I can see your coachman, but I can't see your coach.'

'Yes, Nash, I understand people whizz around like this all day in South Zeal, but I'm not sure Bath is ready, are you?'

The crowd was now quite sizeable, there not in truth being a great deal to do in Bath except take the waters, bathe, play cards, dance a little, and gossip. Dismounting from Tom gingerly, and with a final wave, the doctor made his painful way into the Mineral Hospital, Bath's leading charitable institution for the treatment of the ailing poor, where he was chief physician. The Beau, who had done most of the fund-raising, followed him in with the fond smile of all who are eccentrically befriended.

The Doctor sat down heavily in a chair in the entrance hall and resumed his grimaces and pursed-lip sighs. 'I've nothing personally against your new mode of transport, dear Oliver,' said the Beau. 'But the problem as I see it is that people without our discernment, love of novelty and knowledge of Devon are going to conclude that you can't afford a chair or a carriage, which I wouldn't have thought good for your reputation as the city's leading medical man and acclaimed alleviator of ailments from ague to apoplexy and piles to palsy. How's the gout, by the way?'

'As you can see, Nash, no better than it should be after a generous evening with you. Did we really do a duet of "A Brisk Young Sailor Courted Me"? It was a mistake to try to walk this morning.'

'You need a carriage, Doctor. None of us is getting any younger and your patients really don't want to see you staggering along the street. They like to have a monopoly – or, better, a monotony – of suffering. Nor does one buy beef from a thin butcher or a wig from a blind man. Although in your case…'

'Yes, very good, Beau. Those two scoundrels have decided me: I am going to furnish the hospital with our own chairs!'

'That will be an excellent scheme for the more lame of those in your tender care, dear William, but not quite right for you. A man of your distinction requires distinction from your charges. A carriage, that's the thing!'

'Well, possibly you're right, Nash. And I do have to get to my new sweet country retreat. It's such a lot of trouble, though, a carriage, isn't it? The purchase, the upkeep, the staff and all that fuzzbuzz.'

'Don't worry about that. I can find you a snappy little gig at a very reasonable outlay, plus the Beau's commission, naturally.' (You didn't earn the title of 'Beau' on your looks, but by persuading society that your effrontery was charm, and should be obeyed. But he was indeed charming and had a unique line in brocade, lace and ruffles; and yes, that was indeed a trim of beaver circling his cream hat.)

'I can drive a carriage, Doctor,' said Tom, who had followed the senior pair inside and had been inspecting the hall, unnoticed. 'I was Harvest Champion of South Zeal last year. I finished three cart lengths ahead of Peter Davey, although it was a pity about Jan Stewer's corn, Harry Hawk's hedge, Bill Brewer's barrels, Dan'l Whiddon's marrows and Uncle Tom Cobley and wall.'

'There you are, Oliver,' said the Beau, bowing to Tom with a gentle mockery. 'With young Phaeton here you'll be around Bath in a jiffy, and from the sound of his driving style, you might pick up some extra patients on the way.'

'Oh, very well,' said the Doctor, who in reality quite fancied a carriage, and could see its commercial possibilities, not least some large notices on its side advertising his services *('Got the gout? Feeling peaky? Oliver's the doc to treat 'ee!')*. 'Tom, you're hired. Get down to the kitchen and ask Sally to send up my usual.'

The delighted youth followed the Doctor's gesture and left. The Doctor eyed the Beau with wary affection. 'Don't get me something too fancy, none of your bright colours and jingles and that sort of thing.'

'You have a horse, I take it?'

'A horse? Oh, I see. Don't they come with one?'

'Ah. Leave it to me, my dear Doctor. I am going home to change into my business apparel, achieved by substituting ebony brocade for gold and putting on my waistcoat with the little pound signs. Subtlety, Doctor, subtlety. Tell the lad to meet me in an hour at Mr Lamborghini's, down past the Abbey, fourth on the left.'

In the kitchen, Tom had been making the acquaintance of Sally, the hospital's cook, who was working away at the big table with flour and rolled-up sleeves. Unusually for a cook in such circumstances, Sally was young and very pretty: Tom was particularly taken with the smudge of flour on her right temple where she had brushed away a stray curl with her hand. And by her comestibles. 'I like the look of your cakes,' he said with what he hoped was a cheeky smile.

'Oh, my buns,' she said.

'Buns? Is that what you call them?' replied Tom.

'That's what we call them where I come from.'

'Where is that? I can't quite place your accent, delightful though it is.'

'Wigan.'

'Wigan? The town up in the mysterious north country fabled for its pies?'

'The same. But on Sundays we have buns. Not like here. Here the doctor likes a bun at any time, and insists his patients, rich or poor, have at least three a day. Would you like to try one?'

Tom took a bun from the plate and bit. 'By Crediton crossroads, that's good! And so sweet it's wicked! Can I have another?'

'Aye lad, that's trouble. One bun's no fun, as we say in Wigan. But we're so poor yet proud we prefer to be grim and bear it. Not like round here: the goings-on! I think it must be all the sugar. Which, if you ask me, and even if you don't ask me, is responsible for size of some of them. Most wouldn't fit down our pit even without their pick.'

Sally was now kneading. The colour had risen in her cheeks, which Tom found most attractive.

'Well,' he said. 'The doctor is certainly pretty heavy. Do you think there might possibly be some connection between the eating and drinking and the gout and all their other aches and pains? '

'That's what Mrs Oliver says. The doctor's not convinced, but I think that's mostly because he loves my buns. Five a day, calls them his "usual". They take away the disgusting taste of the Bath water he's so keen on. I expect that's why you've been sent down here. But if Mrs Oliver is against them, they'll go. And if there's to be a bun ban, I'm off. There's money in buns, I reckon, or my name's not Sally, which it is, although I've hopes for changing my last one.'

Now it was Tom's turn to show some colour. 'I do hope you're not going back up north?' he said.

'North's for coming from. No, I've got plans round here.'

Tom's entrancement with Sally's smile, open, direct and just the right touch of naughty, was broken by a shout from the doctor at the top of the stairs. Bath's newest coachman was soon on his way to Mr Lamborghini's.

The coach-builder was tucked away in a mews behind the Abbey. Tom stopped to stare at the fine angels with pudding-bowl haircuts making their way up and down to heaven on their ladders high up the Abbey front, even if no one else crowding round the Pump Room in the sunshine was paying them much heed. Beguiled, he heard the shout of 'Have a care!' moments before Edgar and Silas bumped into him rather too vigorously. 'You can take the boy out of South Zeal, Edgar,' said Silas.

'Odds even!' cried Beau Nash. 'Stop the Sedan. Roughest ride I've had this year. Can't tell my brain from my belly and my arse is positively pummelled.'

'Apologies, Sire,' oiled Silas. 'Uneven road surface and my colleague Edgar is overdue a service. Not to mention ignorant country boys failing to take the correct evasive action. That will be one shilling, please, Sire.'

'A shilling! What's the extra sixpence for?'

'Terms and conditions, Sire. In the case of a collision, liability for damage arising will lie with the carried body or his appointed agents and representatives. Look at that dent the boy's made, Sire. Very expensive.'

'Poppycock! Show me these terms and conditions.'

'I'd like to, Sire, but I can't write.'

'There's sixpence and count yourself lucky I don't set the lad on you.'

Tom, who had now picked himself up, was looking distinctly mean. Silas, complaining that Bath had really gone down lately, and Edgar, still silent, made off at a surprising pace.

'I'm going to have to sort these chairmen out, you know,' said the Beau. 'They'll be wanting performance bonuses next. But fancy bumping into you, young man. Come on, to Lamborghini's.'

'Very droll, Sir. I follow.'

Mr Lamborghini was a small man with a small moustache and the exaggeratedly plausible manner of a certain type of tradesman. The collar of his topcoat was trimmed with velvet and his shoes were of napped leather of the Swedish sort. He sketched a bow of the Italian sort. 'Mr Nash, Sir, a pleasure as ever to welcome you to my humble *garage*, as the French have it. What can I do for you today?'

Mr L's offerings were not that humble, of course: one part of the mews was a stable housing some clearly noble steeds; the other contained a glittering collection of highly polished and richly coloured conveyances, barouches, chaises, and gigs, artfully displayed. The walls were covered in bridles, halters, reins, bits, harnesses, martingales, blankets, whips, horns, boots and every other piece of tack and livery. There was an enticing smell of leather and luxury slightly tempered by Mr L's excessive cologne. The Beau's eye, as it would, fell on a gorgeous thing with cerise quarters and ochre mudguards topped with a cerulean leather hood. 'Ah,' exclaimed Mr L with enthusiasm, 'Sir likes the look of our Landau Gini Grand Tourer Special Edition!'

The Beau went over to the carriage, kicked one of the wheels and checked the suspension by pressing down on the trunk at the back, actions that were no more convincing of specialised knowledge in the area then than they are today.

'Lovely little runner,' said Mr L, with even more enthusiasm. 'Fifty miles to the horse, full warranty, free annual service, yours for only forty-nine guineas and

I'll throw in the horse as well. I'll be ruining myself, of course, but it'll be worth it just to watch Your Lordship pass by on his way out to the country for a spin.'

'Yes, yes, very good, Lamborghini, but the cards haven't been nearly kind enough of late for that sort of outlay. I'm buying for a friend.'

'Of course you are, Sir.'

'I am, damn you. He needs something ideal for short journeys in town and weekend trips to his new second home in Box. None of your folderol, have you got something black, used, one hp, room for him, his wife and a narrow servant?'

'Hmm. If I might make so bold, Your Lordship, your friend might be better off with something more substantial to take him to Box while availing himself of the services of our Sedan friends to negotiate our narrow streets. Luckily, it so happens that I do rather a smart little private Sedan myself, stripes, drinks cabinet and smoked glass. I also have the Sedanette, for the ladies, in pink.'

'He's fallen out with the chairmen, and he already has a coachman,' rejoined the Beau, motioning towards Tom, who was still staring.

'An interesting idea,' said Mr L. 'Putting the coachman before the carriage.' There was a faint but perceptible change in his manner familiar to anyone who has just revealed to an estate agent the modesty of the amount they intend to spend. Mr L mentally balanced possibly upsetting the highly influential Beau against his establishment's monopoly of the fine trade and the imminent arrival of a newly minted carriage-seeking gentleman from

Chingford who had done exceedingly well in the area of waste disposal. 'In that case, my lord, I think it might be better if my assistant helped you...Luigi!'

Trailing scent and disappointment, Mr L withdrew to a small sanctum at the back of the mews to await the arrival of Mr Chingford. A large youth appeared, tightly fitted into what were clearly Mr L's hand-me-downs. 'Yus?' he asked, or rather demanded. The question was preceded and followed by a sniff and pronounced in tones that owed more to Frome than Rome. The Beau explained again the doctor's requirements; Luigi sniffed again, more lengthily, bowed as much as his jacket would allow and suggested they should follow him to the Diligently Owned by One Mature Gentlewoman Salon.

A short time later, following a visit round the back of the mews and several more sniffs of increasing vigour and volume as the Beau demonstrated exactly why he was generally successful at the tables, Tom was driving a dog-cart of exemplary dullness and remarkably modest value back to the Hospital, while the Beau was striding towards Harrison's Lower Assembly Rooms for his daily cards, drinks and dalliances (and, in the way of beaux and gamblers, not revealing his, how shall we say, especial interest in the finances of the establishment). Ah, Bath, what splendid shades there are in your flimsy, flashy past!

Halting his new (to him) carriage in Bear Yard at the side of the hospital, Tom went inside to find his new employer. A group of patients was being assembled for the daily trip to the hot bath, distinguished by the sewn badges which allowed them entrance to the bath (and identified them to be turned away if they tried to shuffle off into a convenient hostelry). Those that weren't limping displayed the various skin conditions such as impetigo and psoriasis more generally known in these times as leprosy. They were of course grateful for the charity bestowed by the great and good of Bath which secured them a bed and treatment (and kept them off the streets in inconvenient and deterring view of visitors), but they could not be accused of looking happy. A young woman was shepherding them towards the door. After they'd left, she came over to Tom, brisk and enquiring. He noticed that her eyes were the same shade as the sea at Maidencombe around noon on a June day. 'Hmm,' she said. 'Over-ruddy complexion for a young man, could be an excitation of the skin or some perturbation of the blood. Follow me and I'll get you examined.'

Tom decided against telling her it was because he was blushing. 'I'm a country boy,' he said. 'It's all the open air. I'm not ill, I'm the doctor's new coachman. Are you a doctor, too?'

The woman laughed, which Tom thought had a most pleasing effect, especially in the contrast to the (equally fetching) severity she had been exhibiting so far. 'A doctor! Haven't you noticed? I'm a woman! Are you sure about your face? It's almost purple now! Men like to keep the official doctoring to themselves to prevent them from being shown up by our superior gifts. One day they'll come to their senses but I wouldn't hold your breath. Especially you, with that colour. I'm the matron here, Olive Whitlock.'

'Olive, that's an unusual name.'

'My father is very keen on them. Mostly in gin. But I can't stand around here all day. I've got patients to order about.'

'Well, it has been a pleasure to make your acquaintance, I'm sure, Mrs Whitlock. Do you know where I might find the doctor?'

'In his consulting room. He has had some grave news. You might have noticed a certain gloom among the patients, too.'

Tom made his way to the consulting room, where he found the doctor sitting at his desk, forlorn. 'Ah, Tom, how goes the day?' he asked, plainly distracted.

'Very well, Sir. Mr Nash acquired a splendid carriage for you which is now outside in Bear Yard. Smart little runner which I will keep in the old stables at the back of the hospital. I was also wondering if I should have some sort of livery, Sir. This old coat would be more at home on a baker's round.'

'Baker's round! That's it, Tom – baker! – that's our trouble! Sally has left us!'

Tom was disturbed by this news for a variety of reasons. 'What happened, Sir?'

'On Mrs Oliver's instructions, I told Sally I much enjoyed her "buns", but asked her if she could come up with a comestible that didn't apply quite so much *avoirdupois* to my waist and that of my patients. Well, she took a most unreasonable position and starting shouting something about, as far as I could make out – you will recall that she came from the far regions – "Bloody

Health and Pastry". Then she took her apron off, threw it to the floor and stormed out and off. No more of Sally's buns, Tom – that was bad enough. But to have lost Sally entirely!'

'Is there no one else who could cook, Sir? I would volunteer but my gravy has been held to be even lumpier than the road to Cullompton. Mother says men won't really be interested in cooking until someone invents a fancy foreign name for cook.'

'Your mother is clearly a very wise woman but that doesn't help me in the current predicament. I'm sure Mrs Whitlock is a wonderful cook but she's far too busy running the hospital. I often worry about her going off to get married. What would we do? And now Sally! I've never been more in need of a bun!'

'Currant predicament! That's very good, Sir! Current…Buns!'

The Doctor continued to look puzzled, so Tom moved conversation swiftly on. 'Isn't Mrs Whitlock married, Sir?'

'You seem interested, Tom! No, she's not married. There's some confusion over these titles. Mister and Mistress are the senior equivalents of Master and Miss, but Mistress or Mrs also denotes a position of authority, while unmarried ladies of the higher classes are increasingly referred to as Miss. It would be much simpler if there was one simple title, Ms, say, but English society depends on meaningless and impenetrable distinctions, so don't hold your breath, especially as you're quite red in the face already. The only answer to the current pressing predicament is for you to go over to Queen Square and bring my cook over there over here. Off you go! And don't spare the, er, horse!'

Dr Oliver's house, at the north-western corner of the Square, was as imposing as a house designed by John Wood, the city's principal architect and guiding spirit, tended to be, although this didn't prevent certain elements of Bath society sniffing about the insufficient antecedents of anyone who lived in a recent construction. The Doctor's remunerative position as Bath's most fashionable physician, gained by his friendship with Wood, Ralph Allen, Beau Nash and other city fathers, guaranteed such stuff, as did his whiggish views. But his kindness was delivered unstintingly to all and was responsible for his success in treating and keeping his patients. Tom, oblivious to all of this bar, the kindness and a certain vaguery, was still a little surprised to discover, after a couple of embarrassed enquiries, that the Square was about two minutes from the hospital. Grateful that there was no sign of Edgar and Silas, he halted the carriage outside the Oliver establishment and went through the servants' entrance, which led to the kitchen, empty but for a young girl of an extra fine complexion and large amounts of lustrousness. She was kneading.

'Hello,' she said, in an accent that delightfully conjured jingling sleighs and tall firs, 'I'm Britt. You must be the new coachman of the doctor.'

'Stap my chitterlings, how did you know that?'

Britt smiled at him. She was the third young woman who had smiled at him over the past hours and he was no nearer getting used to it. 'Ah, we who have travelled from the far have our ways of the mystery. And you're carrying a whip.'

This was the third time that Tom had blushed over the past hours, but the first time for feeling silly. 'Yes, of course, foolish, I'm looking for the cook.'

'You have found her. Trained under Madame Berrynova in Kursk and a how-you-say dab hand with the pan rattling if I do say this myself.'

Tom dealt with the fourth time. 'Sorry, yes, of course you are. The doctor wants you over at the hospital.'

'Yes, I thought as muchness. Sally, she has gone off to open a shop for the buns. The doctor will now be requiring of immediately a Britt bun which is not so evidently fattening as the buns of Sally but still as satisfying. And Britt Bakoff, she is best the girl to do it. This is what I am working on now: the currants, the raisins and the sultanas will be providing the sweetness, the jiffy-jiff, while at the same stroke of the clock reducing the hill of the sugar, the iffy-iff. Here, be carrying my bowl and we over to the hospital will go.'

Tom, much affected by the girl's determination, directness and, to be honest, a smile that would even have earned a discount from Silas, did as he was bid. It was at this moment that Mrs Oliver came bustling in. Tom, though young, was already surprised at how rarely people match up to imaginings of them before they are met. He had conceived of Mrs Oliver as a forbidding presence, but she was much the same shape as the doctor, beaming broadly. 'Ah, young man,' she said, looking at Tom and the bowl. 'Are you a scullion? I seem to remember that the young pretender Lambert Simnel was employed as a scullion by King Henry after his rebellion failed, but I had no idea we were grand enough to have one! On the other hand, as the mistress of this house, I would have hired you, so you can't be.'

'I'm Tom Atkins, the new coachman, Mistress. I was just helping Britt.'

'The new coachman! Wonderful! I didn't even know we had a coach. In fact, I didn't even know we needed one.'

'It's on account of the doctor's gout, Mistress, and getting to your new country home.'

'Country home? Gracious me, that must be a birthday surprise!'

Tom really was spending a tremendous amount of time blushing. Mrs Oliver looked benignly at him over her spectacles and then burst out laughing.

'Don't worry, Tom, it's a joke! I like my jokes, don't I, Britt? The doctor much enjoys them as well. I'm not sure how well the latest one about getting rid of Sally's buns went down, though.'

'Not too well of the jolly kind, Mistress,' said Britt. 'Sally has walked out and Tom is to take me over to the hospital in the speedy way with my new mix of the bun.'

'Oh, dear,' said Mrs Oliver, who, it has to be said, didn't look overly concerned. 'We have Mr Ralph Allen for supper, too. He's bound to be late, though. He always is, which is odd, given that he's Bath's postmaster and postmaster for most elsewhere, come to that. I always call him the late Mr Allen. If you don't get back in time, I'll serve him coffee and tell him he's just missed a feast.'

So, with the beautiful Britt and the mixing bowl behind him, Tom embarked on the short trundle back to the hospital. It was now the beginning of one of those late summer evenings that have always been Bath's delight, when the scents and sights of the day calmly give way to those of the night. Last visitors lingered in the dying light in the Orange Grove and the newly modelled gardens surrounding Harrison's, where the Beau–, as charming as ever, providing one knew how to behave–, lay in wait at the table. Elsewhere, fashionable and unfashionable men and women studied themselves in looking glasses in preparation, while outside Edgar and Silas were in familiar altercation with a plainly disgruntled fare. Dr Oliver was taking more time than he should with his charitable work at the hospital. Olive Whitlock was slightly less brisk and more pensive than usual. Ralph Allen, busy making the mail arrive on time and arranging the quarrying of more of the honeyed stone with which John Wood was building his elegant and mysterious marvels, was indeed going to be late. Mrs Oliver was sitting at a window in Queen Square by a candle and chuckling over *Moll Flanders*. Across the Square, by another candle and window, John Wood was engrossed in his theories that Bladud and the druids built the first Bath on the model of Stonehenge and Stanton Drew. Over in New King Street, William Herschel was preparing for another night in the back garden with his excellent telescope (later he will have something very interesting to tell his sister Caroline). Mr Lamborghini was still muttering, but Luigi, somewhat distracted of late, was paying little attention. A Roman centurion passed by the Baths but, as usual, no one noticed.

And next? Well, predictably, Britt's bun was a triumph, equally as popular as Sally's northern delight. So popular that it became known as the Bath Bun (after a short spell as the Kursk Crumpet). Sadly, too, it was equally successful at putting weight on the doctor and his patients. Eventually and inevitably, the doctor had to bow (only figuratively, given his waist) to sense and science and ban the Bath Bun as well. Enter the always eminently sensible Olive Whitlock, who came up with the beguiling and far less fattening biscuit named, in her honour, the Bath Olive. Word of mouth, coincidence and prejudices being what they were and are, her triumph soon became better known as the Bath Oliver, after her employer. Which didn't work out too badly, as the doctor, always a gentleman, bequeathed the recipe to her husband (such were the times) along with £100 and (a nice touch, suggested by Mrs Oliver) ten sacks of flour. Olive and her husband then set up a shop in Green Street and made rather a lot of money.

Her husband was, of course, Tom. Sally married her sweetheart, Luigi, whose real name was George Lunn; they did pretty well, too. Britt became something of a celebrity – 'the Great Britt Bakov' – training the cooks of the gentry and marrying one of the doctor's wealthier patients who could not live without her buns, the said gent from Chingford.

The Beau played his part in regulating and licensing the Sedan chairmen. After a number of complaints, Edgar and Silas left the trade but contrived to make a living hiring themselves out as uniformed footmen who could make halls and gardens look larger than they were if tall Edgar stood at one end and small Silas at the other. I almost forgot to mention that Mr Lamborghini was not Italian but Olive's father, Frederick Whitlock. There have to be some unhappy endings, but I am still sad to report that the Beau died in straitened circumstances; nevertheless, I doubt he would have exchanged any of it for something duller.

Afterword

SOME OF THIS IS TRUE. WILLIAM OLIVER (1695–
1764) was a Cornishman who, helped by the patronage
of Richard Nash, Ralph Allen and John Wood, became
Bath's most sought-after physician in the first half of the
eighteenth century, when, with the patronage of Good
Queen Anne and her gout, the city and its waters became
highly fashionable once more after, oh, 1300 years. All of
them helped found the Royal Mineral Water Hospital,
a charity aimed at helping the numbers of indigent
rheumatics and others who flocked to Bath to beg and
seek a cure as its fame rose. It also took them off the streets
and stopped them frightening wealthier visitors. Oliver
became its chief physician. According to the Dictionary of
National Biography, 'He was generally admitted to have
been an eminently sensible man, and one also of a most
compassionate and benevolent nature.' There is a splendid
picture on display at the hospital of Oliver and its surgeon,
Jeremiah 'Jerry' Pierce, with patients. It is by WILLIAM
HOARE (1707–92), the great Bath portrait painter, who

was a patron and governor of the hospital. Henry Hoare, from the banking side of the family and purchaser of the great nearby estate, Stourhead, was among the first to suggest founding the hospital; he and his bank, C Hoare & Co, continued to be great supporters. MRS WHITLOCK was indeed the first matron; but her first name was Hester, and she spent nineteen years at the hospital rather than inventing the Bath Oliver and marrying Tom Atkins.

Oliver lived in Queen Square and had a country retreat at Box. He himself suffered from gout for many years and wrote a treatise on the condition entitled 'A practical essay on the use and abuse of warm bathing in gouty cases,' where he wrote that in his 'happy experience' Bath's warm water could generally relieve and, with the correct supervision, even cure the malady. He was also instrumental in establishing the popularity of drinking the waters as a health cure.

He is supposed to have confected and prescribed the sweet delight we know as the Bath Bun. It was so popular that his patients put on large amounts of weight, leading the doctor to come up with a healthier alternative, the Bath Oliver biscuit. Legend is persistent that towards the end of his life he gave the recipe to his coachman, Atkins, along with £100 and ten sacks of flour. Atkins did open a shop selling the biscuits in Green Street which became a great success. A link has yet to emerge between Oliver and another of Bath's premier gifts, the Sally Lunn, a brioche of a bun said, among several other explanations, to have arrived with a Huguenot refugee called Solange Luyon. But there is always a chance, as it was only in 1937 that the original recipes were recovered from a secret cupboard in the medieval building which, by remarkable serendipity, a new owner was preparing to open as Sally Lunn's house and bakery.

RALPH ALLEN (1693–1764) was also from Cornwall. A precocious youth, he worked his way in the Post Office from St Columb to Exeter to Bath, and was appointed postmaster in the city at the age of nineteen. Not content with this, he began buying up contracts to deliver the post all over the country, making a large amount of money by introducing routes which avoided London. Not content with that, he then made a second fortune from the wonderfully honeyed Bath limestone, which he sourced and quarried with a view to selling it to London, then in a rush of development. When it was deemed too soft for London, Allen, unabashed, determined to develop Bath instead, linking up with the inspired architect, John Wood, to build and plan Queen Square, the Circus and the Crescent. Wood also designed Allen's great house, Prior Park, on the hill west of the city, 'to see all Bath and be seen by all Bath'. There he entertained such as Alexander Pope and Henry Fielding, who modelled Squire Allworthy, Tom Jones's amiable foster father, on Allen, a man of much philanthropy as well as profit. He is buried in a most splendid pyramid of a mausoleum in the churchyard at Claverton, close to his quarry at Combe Down. Pope paid this tribute to his patron in the Epilogue to his Satires,

> *'Let humble Allen, with an awkward shame*
> *Do good by stealth, and blush to find it fame'.*

Allen hated it.

JOHN WOOD (1704–1754) is another Bath figure of uncertain origin, but he was probably born in the city, the son of a local builder. His obsessive enthusiasms, most notably architecture, antiquarianism and alchemy, came together in his master works: Queen Square, the King's Circus and the Royal Crescent. Their classical elegance was inspired by Andrea Palladio, the great Renaissance architect, while their layout and embellishments ensued from Wood's mythic vision of an ancient Bath founded around 500 BC by Bladud: king, magus and arch-druid.

Wood's ancient Bath was an enormous metropolis, stretching from the standing stones of Stanton Drew, marking what was a druid academy, to Wookey Hole, twenty-one miles south, hewn by the druids for secret ceremonies, via West Harptree, a school for, naturally, harpists. Beechen Cliff is Camaludonum, Camelot, while Lansdown is Mount Badon, where, as we shall see, Arthur was supposed to have fought his great battle. The druid worship of the sun and the moon is said to be reflected by the mighty Circus as the sun and the great Crescent as the moon. The Crescent, as befits the cold moon, was sparely decorated; the Circus, as the hot sun, was not, and much rewards a tour examining the masks and symbols on its friezes. Rays of light, thunderbolts, suns, moons, triangles, beehives, serpents devouring themselves, a phoenix, blasted oaks, roses, skulls, a wolf howling at the moon: this is a riot of Rosicrucianism, druidry, Freemasonry and alchemy, with an added dash of Templars and the Bible topped by the stone acorns on the pediment above. Consider, too, the theory that the Square, the Circus and the Crescent viewed from above form a key, a prime Masonic symbol.

Little wonder another theory holds that this jostling gallery of images drawn from any number of mystical persuasions is an attempt to display a unity of beliefs, the answer to everything, the philosopher's stone sought so obsessively by the alchemists, who, of course, included Wood's hero, Isaac Newton. Alternatively, it may just be a tremendous jeu d'esprit *from Wood and his son, also John, who followed his father and completed the Circus and the Crescent. Do not underestimate the penchant of architects to introduce subtle suggestions into their work: not everyone knows, for example, that Midsummer Boulevard, the high street of that gridded and proudly new town, Milton Keynes, is aligned so that the rays of the summer solstice sunrise can reflect dazzlingly in the mirrored walls of the railway station.*

You will not be surprised to learn that Wood was a difficult man, falling out with, among others, Ralph Allen, his sometime partner. Nor that what he achieved in Bath is but a part of what he wanted to do with the city, including re-creating what he believed to be a great British forum where now stands Nando's and Greggs, complete with a mighty octangular basin which would have created a port. Such dreams. Believe what you will; marvel at what is.

I have stretched a little to include WILLIAM HERSCHEL (1738–1822) and CAROLINE HERSCHEL (1750–1848), refugees, musicians, and astronomers, as they did not arrive in Bath until shortly after Beau Nash died. Forgive me, and enjoy a visit to the museum commemorating them in their old house, which, among other fascinating things, explains how between them the

Herschels sang, played, composed and directed Bath's music and ran a millinery business while also discovering Uranus. Herschel went on to detect infrared radiation, while Caroline, a formidable astronomer in her own right, discovered several comets and nebulae.

RICHARD 'BEAU' NASH (1674–1761) is one of those many figures, like John Wesley, with whom he often clashed, whose power and personality demand explanation by a recorded and moving image, are lost on the page. How else to account for Nash's influence and sway over Bath, where he convinced the lowest and the highest to conform to his clever ways of regulating the infant resort? He arrived in the city in 1705 as a failed soldier and lawyer now making his living as a gamester at the card tables, attracted by the potential pickings from the nobility and nobility apers and chasers who had followed the late Queen Anne and others of her family. This novel mixing of the upper and middle classes demanded a new set of rules: and Nash was ideally suited to introduce and enforce them, as there could be no better social observer and arbiter than a professional gambler of obscure origins and a good (Oxford) education. His opportunity came when Bath's then 'Master of Ceremonies', a Captain Webster, also a gamester but rather too much of a drinker, was challenged to a duel and killed by an unhappy loser at his table. Nash, his deputy, took over and, rather in the manner of a sheriff in the Wild(er) West, began to enforce some more civilised behaviour, but with charm and chutzpah rather than rifle and revolver. Swords, dangerous at both the tables and when dancing, were outlawed, as were boots, often worn by country gentry immediately arrived.

Nash forced the upper classes to mingle with their supposed inferiors, even ensuring noble dancers didn't disdain to touch those less lucky by birth. He ended all dances at 11pm exactly in a bow to invalids needing their rest. Recognising that public life rather than private entertainment was crucial to the city's success, he encouraged the rebuilding of the Pump Room and new assembly rooms. Subscriptions to these and much else subsidised the entertainments.

Nash was not only generous with his advice but also with his charity and that of others: he was as likely to be collecting for some good cause – as with Dr Oliver's hospital – as he was to be enforcing his rules. He was celebrated for whimsical cancellation of gambling debts of the young and foolish and for his private cautions against chancers and rash romances: 'The great error lies in imagining every fellow with a laced coat to be a gentleman.'

But, in all this, there was ever a certain sense of ridicule and slightly mocking indulgence, as in his title, 'King of Bath'.

His pomp and purple lasted until the 1740s when changed circumstance changed his circumstance. The invention of new card games to circumvent anti-gambling legislation led him to take an undisclosed share in profits at both Bath and his satellite operation, Tunbridge Wells. His reputation and his finances never recovered after this was revealed in a court case he unwisely brought against unscrupulous partners.

He also made the cardinal error of the man of fashion: living too long. His last years were ones of increasing derision and decreasing income. Instead of witticisms, he handed out tracts defending himself. Where he had been respected, at the Pump Room and in the assembly rooms, he was now resented, an old and querulous bore.

And yet, as is also not uncommon, when he died, there was an outpouring of respect and encomia. Oliver Goldsmith, in his beguiling biography of the Beau, wrote:

'The day after he died, the Mayor of Bath called the corporation together, where they granted fifty pounds towards burying their sovereign with proper respect. After the corpse had lain four days, it was conveyed to the abbey church in the city, with a solemnity somewhat peculiar to his character. About five the procession moved from his house, the charity girls two and two preceded, next the boys of the charity school singing a solemn occasional hymn... The masters of the assembly-rooms followed as chief mourners, the beadles of that hospital, which he had contributed so largely to endow, went next, and last of all, the poor patients themselves, the lame, the emaciated, and the feeble, followed their old benefactor to his grave, shedding unfeigned tears, and lamenting themselves in him.

'The crowd was so great, that not only the streets were filled, but, as one of the journals... expresses it, "even the tops of the houses were covered with spectators, each thought the occasion affected themselves most; as when a real king dies, they asked each other, 'where shall we find such another?' Sorrow sat upon every face, and even children lisped *that their Sovereign was no more. The awfulness of the solemnity made the deepest impression on the minds of the distressed inhabitants. The peasant discontinued his toil, the ox rested from the plough, all nature seemed to sympathise with their lots, and the muffled bells rung a peal of Bob Major."'*

And this was his old friend, Dr Oliver: 'With all these... foibles, follies, faults or frailties, it will be difficult to point out among his contemporary kings of the earth more than one who hath fewer [of them], or less pernicious to mankind.'

The Beau's passing marked that of Bath as the non pareil *of high fashion. Nash's success in introducing an element of egalitarianism did not survive his force and charm; it is, in any case, difficult to see the point of the upper classes if they cannot look down. Tobias Smollett expressed this better than most when he had his Squire, Matthew Bramble, declare Bath to be a place where a very inconsiderable proportion of genteel people were lost in a mob of impudent plebeians, including 'Mr Bullock, an eminent cow keeper of Tottenham' (I assume Mr Bullock was acquainted with our friend from Chingford). Royalty, toffs and the ton began to look for more exclusive resorts, often by the seaside. Bath began to lose its raff as retired officers and clergymen arrived in their numbers and stead. The Age of Austen was upon it.*

See:

> *Queen Square, The Circus, The Royal Crescent (Number One is a museum re-creating the period 1776–96: no1royalcrescent.org.uk).*

St John's Place and Saw Close.

Beau Nash lived in houses on either side and on the site of the Theatre Royal in Saw Close, which opened in 1805. The grander, when he was in his pomp, is now The Garrick's Head pub and restaurant. The other, also now a restaurant, belonged to his eccentric and wonderfully named mistress, Juliana Popjoy; the Beau moved there in his final, less glorious years. A casino has now opened on the other side of the road, with, naturally, a Beau Nash Suite. Disappointingly, the bingo hall farther down has now closed. Ms Popjoy, according to account, spent her final years living in a tree near Warminster. But it is Saw Close she haunts.

Dr Oliver's hospital, subsequently the Royal National Hospital for Rheumatic Disease, but forever known to Bath as The Min, is set to become a hotel. The small but enjoyable museum featuring the special chair designed for patients is being developed as the Bath Museum of Medicine in Great Pulteney Street, which will also display many of The Min's fine paintings (bathmedicalmuseum.org). Bath's conveyances have been numerous and varied, from the Sedan chair favoured by Silas and Edgar to smaller poled versions used for bathers, whose needs were successively catered for by wheeled chairs, evolving by the nineteenth century into the most familiar Bath Chair, manufactured in the city by firms such as Austin Dawson and James Heath (but not, sadly, Lamborghini). Fares charged by the chairmen did not follow the model of Silas and Edgar. Within the old city walls, it was sixpence; outside, a shilling or more, depending on distance. Waiting time was also charged. By the middle of the eighteenth century, the charge was a straight sixpence for up to 500 yards, one shilling up to a mile. A rowdy protest of the gilet jaune *variety over new regulations in 1793 resulted in Bath Corporation swiftly agreeing to a charge for hilly ground at sixpence for each 300 yards instead of the old 500. Opinion differs on the degree of bad behaviour by coachmen, though not on the need to get out of their way. I would like the theory that 'Cheerio!' derives from their warning cries – 'Chair-ho!' – to be true.*

Prior Park *itself is now a school. The garden is owned by the National Trust, and shares the fine views of the city. Five minutes away is the Trust's Bath Skyline, a six-mile circular walk above the city. (nationaltrust.org.uk).*

Bath Postal Museum, *27 Northgate Street, BA1 1AJ. Independent, small but very informative about Bath's key role in the rapid improvements to the Royal Mail, featuring Ralph Allen, and JOHN PALMER (1742–1818), deviser of the Mail Coaches, which increased security and cut journey times around the country by more than a half until they were superseded by the railways. The racy essay of the road by that most talented writer, Bath resident and noted recreational drug user, THOMAS DE QUINCEY (1785–1859), is well worth the read. Palmer became Comptroller General of the Post Office, and later was twice Mayor of Bath and its MP from 1801–08. His entrepreneurial and logistical skills were honed running his family's Orchard Street theatre, Bath's first, for which he obtained a royal patent, making it the Theatre Royal, where trod such as Mrs Siddons, travelling daily between Bath and his Bristol Theatre Royal. (bathpostalmuseum. org.uk, oldtheatreroyal.com).*

Herschel Museum of Astronomy, 19, New King Street, BA1 2BL (herschelmuseum.org).

The Grand Pump Room, Abbey Church Yard, BA1 1LY, was opened in 1795, replacing the earlier building commissioned by Nash. It forms part of the Roman baths complex, which shouldn't work but does thanks to an inspired combination of Georgian and Victorian self-importance (romanbaths.co.uk).

The Lower Assembly Rooms, operated by Thomas Harrison in alliance with Beau Nash, were situated on what is now Parade Gardens. They fell out of fashion and closed after the opening of the Upper Assembly Rooms in 1771. Later destroyed in a fire, they were replaced by a grand new building housing the estimable Bath Royal Literary and Scientific Institution until its removal to Queen Square (on the site of Dr Oliver's house) in 1932 in response to yet another redevelopment. Bath has been notoriously unsentimental about the buildings of earlier generations since Saxon times. But there is at least a plaque in memory of the dancing, gambling and drama on the parapet on Grand Parade above Parade Gardens, BA1 1EE.

Read:

The Life of Beau Nash, *by Oliver Goldsmith, 1762.*

The Myth-Maker, John Wood, 1704–1754, *by Kirsten Elliott, 2004.*

The English Mail-Coach, *by Thomas De Quincey, 1849.*

Bath, *by Edith Sitwell, 1932.*

Chair Transport in Bath:The Sedan Era, *by Trevor Fawcett, 1988.*

Diseased, Douched and Doctored, *by Roger Rolls, 2012.*

Mr Bennet Goes Out

ON BALANCE, AND AFTER A PROPER CONSIDERATION, it is quite fair to say that Mr Bennet was not entirely enamoured of Bath. The place was noisy and frivolous and, despite an outward devotion to its healing waters, in reality existed only for meeting people, perhaps his least favoured activity. Moreover, it did not contain his library.

Yet, every so often, a certain invisible but invincible pressure would be applied against that cherished sanctum's door, a constant chorus, both wavering and unwavering, of concerted supplication; an orgy of entreaty that demanded a firm response. Mrs Bennet and her daughters wanted to go to Bath. And Mr Bennet's firm response was to agree with them.

For though he might appear more than a touch inconsistent, inclined to vacillation, and even weak, Mr Bennet was in fact an accomplished tactician, schooled in the arts of both soldiers and politicians from ancient days to his: the hours in the library had not been wasted, despite what his wife and daughters might claim (although he would yield to none over his forty minutes with eyes firmly closed after luncheon). His studies of Caesar, Augustus and any number of Greeks had led him to a lively appreciation of what has come to be known as 'the bigger picture'. And this, for Mr Bennet, was to be left alone as much as possible. To achieve it, he was willing to surrender his Hertfordshire seclusion in favour of the occasional foray to the delights of Bath; but only after his family had fully realised the extent of his sacrifice and the rarity of the treat it would provide. In this way he could also continue to complain as usual about most of his family while entertaining himself with what he fancied were highly amusing sallies against them.

Some called him a cynic. But like most of the type, he used his world-weary and well-worked witticisms to conceal a deep sentimentality, especially about himself. He thought the world most remiss in not recognising his singular merits despite making no efforts to promote them. He thought he had been most unlucky in his wife, whose interests and intellect were not as his, even though it had been his own free choice to marry her because she was so damn sexy. He thought his daughters less than loving even though he kept them at a distance with his teasing and mock-despair of them. He thought his estate disappointingly unproductive when he took no measures to improve it. And so he spent most of his time in his library, waiting for he was not sure what, while working occasionally on various projects yet to be properly pursued.

Nevertheless, he had his merits. He was clever, with an unusual turn of mind. He could indeed be witty. He was loyal, given to acts of quiet kindness, and surprisingly tolerant of his wife, who could be in turns repetitive, irritating, irritating and repetitive; for her part, she tolerated his mockery because she remembered his tenderness in private and still hoped to enjoy it again, even though she was now not so damn sexy. And so to Bath, this September, to a house in Gay Street, taken, after some protracted wilful-monarch-wily-chancellor negotiations, for two months rather than three, so that Mr Bennet would at least have time to settle back into life at Longbourn before having to evade the Yule tiresomenesses. His one requirement, apart from a ban on mentioning the forthcoming visit at meals, was, of course, a library; or rather, a room in which he could closet himself with a few of his favourite books, brought for the purpose, and from which, of course, he intended to exit only for sustenance and (more) sleep.

*

As EXPLAINED, THIS WAS NOT MR BENNET'S FIRST VISIT to what he liked to call, 'the fashionable watering hole whose description would be more faithfully retailed if the aqueous adjective were to be omitted'. His earliest encounter with the Queen of the West had been more voluntary, and, as he often reflected in either library, more than somewhat significant.

That had been in his early twenties, when, after an averagely dissolute and industrious time at Oxford, he developed a certain lowness of spirit, which, try as he might, mostly as a vigorous member of the Hertfordshire Hunt, he couldn't shake off. His father, not a man given to easy sympathy or sentiment, pronounced that the best remedy would be to embrace something that would provide real and proper worry, such as a wife; his mother, a gentler soul, advised a trip to Bath, where the waters were able to relieve any condition known to trouble, or even slightly irritate, humanity. And so Mr Bennet decided to follow both pieces of parental wisdom and took lodgings (in Gay Street, where he liked always to return, as he did not entirely follow his father in the matter of emotion).

He resided in Bath for several months during the autumn of 177—. The most conspicuous of these days came early in the second week of his stay. Towards evening, despairing a little of the company of some distant relatives, more tea and certainly of any more water, he entered the Pelican on Walcot Street, a comfortable, darkly panelled inn familiar to those times, heavy with that lost essence of mingled woodsmoke, horse, tobacco, sawdust, and stale beer. Having ordered a Madeira, he became aware, as he could hardly fail to, of three men at the other side of the saloon. One was a large and plain fellow dressed plainly and with a wig that had clearly seen no powder since at least the first George had traded in his temporality; the next was dark, lively and not as plump as the first; the third was yet darker, with a gravity carried lightly.

To report that they were engaged in lively conversation would be incorrect, as their intercourse consisted of a booming monologue from the first man, occasionally relieved by either a question or uproarious laughter from the second, who was taking notes in a small book. The third spoke rarely but raised his eyes to the ceiling frequently. Mr Bennet was somewhat at a loss to understand the laughter, as much of what the first man was saying seemed to him to fall into those contrasts that initially seem clever but on closer examination prove to be statements of the sanguinarily discernible, better known to a plainer age as the bleeding obvious. Thus, 'He that will enjoy the brightness of sunshine, must quit the coolness of the shade,' and 'It is a most mortifying reflection for a man to consider what he has done, compared to what he might have done.' There seemed, too, to be some acknowledgement of this from the second man, who had taken to following his laughter with a wink at Mr Bennet. The third man resolutely avoided Mr Bennet's eye.

At length, after another *aperçu* which seemed to have no relevance other than to some long list in the large head below the unloved wig – 'When making your choice in life, do not neglect to live' – the first man turned to Mr Bennet and announced, 'Good day to you, Sir, I look upon every day to be lost in which I do not make a new acquaintance. I am Dr Samuel Johnson of Lichfield and wide repute.'

'Good day to you, Sir. I am Anthony Bennet. I imagine I am as well known in Longbourn, Hertfordshire, as you are in Lichfield, Staffs, but I cannot claim to any wider report, even in Bath, where I am but lately arrived and am unconvinced of a desire to stay very much longer.'

'Well, Sir! Tiring of Bath already! I have to tell you that when a man is tired of Bath, he is tired of life; for there is in Bath all that life can afford.'

'He remarks that of everywhere we go,' said the blacker man. 'Last week we were in Lower Peover.'

The first man, to give him his due, joined in the laughter. The second proposed from the side of his mouth in a low voice that the third, whom he addressed as Mr Barber, might perhaps be better engaged in seeking out more refreshment for Mr Bennet and their party. Mr Barber raised his eyes once more and went off.

'I will introduce myself, Sir, to preserve the doctor's astounding intellect from such trifling concerns.' The doctor smiled the indulgent smile of a man used to being indulged and made a small gesture with one of his large hands, setting off a cloud of dust from his sleeve.

'I am James Boswell, of Auchinleck, Edinburgh and London, lawyer, writer, man about town and general fossicker after novelty, entertainment and knowledge. I have determined that I shall demonstrate to and preserve for history the doctor's character and wisdoms, without, obviously, any thought of myself. His renown shall be my reward.' Here Boswell winked at Mr Bennet again.

The doctor let forth a large belch, commenting, 'Better without than within.' Boswell did not make a note. 'Where's my drink? Where's Mr Barber?'

There then followed a particularly lengthy digression by the doctor on the numerous occasions when tardiness had produced unfortunate results, including Venus arriving too late to save Adonis from the wild boar, and

Thucydides failing to save Amphipolis from the Spartans for the same reason. The doctor addressed these remarks to a spot high up on the opposite wall, which allowed Boswell to confide in his low tone to Mr Bennet that Mr Barber was a native of Jamaica who had arrived in England as a slave and had been freed by the doctor, 'although it is a straitened form of liberty, serving the tetchy sage'.

Mr Barber returned, bearing port for the doctor, claret for Boswell and Madeira for Mr Bennet. The doctor took a hefty swig, sighed with heavy satisfaction, and pronounced, 'Ah, Sir! Claret is the liquor for boys; port, for men; but he who aspires to be a hero must drink brandy. In the first place, brandy is most grateful to the palate; and then brandy will do soonest for a man what drinking *can* do for him. There are, indeed, few who are able to drink brandy. That is a power rather to be wished for than attained'.

Mr Bennet, emboldened by another sip of Madeira, responded, 'Two things, Sir. Why are you then drinking port? And why is there a slice of orange in it? Is that not likely to leave you at the mercy of suggestions that you most closely resemble the chemise of a doxy of ample proportion?'

The doctor narrowed his eyes then raised his right eyebrow so vigorously that another cloud of dust rose. 'It is not a slice of orange, Sir; it is a slice of orange peel, excellent for the digestion and far removed from any ornamental purpose that might secure the notoriously uncertain attention and approbation of the more decorative members of our humble species. Have you seen a woman drink port, Sir? It is not done well; but you are surprised to find it done at all.'

Mr Bennet at that age was not quite so slavishly devoted to the last word, and contented himself with having so excited the great man, who now continued: 'As for a hero, no man is such to his valet'.

Mr Barber, who had been mouthing silently in accompaniment to the doctor's remarks, permitted himself a smile and desisted. 'Nor am I to anyone. A hero moves from battle to battle: I move merely from book to book, coffee house to coffee house, tavern to tavern. There are far more writers than heroes, but the same number of great writers. And the chances of a great writer being a hero are the same as a hero entering through that door now.'

At which point, inevitably, the door was flung open. But instead of a burly figure with a gleaming eye, bass voice and appropriate swagger, there appeared a pale, slight, slender and small youth of tender years who, entirely unmoved by the laughter his arrival had provoked, enquired of the doctor where he might get a large brandy in a voice as treble-pitched as it was clearly used to being noticed.

Mr Barber got to his feet, elegantly but with more urgency than before. 'You're a navy man, Sir? I have also had that honour. I was a landsman for a short period, and much enjoyed it until my friend and mentor, Dr Johnson here, decided I would be much better served serving him than serving the king.'

'Indeed I did,' responded the doctor. 'No man will be a sailor who has contrivance enough to get himself into a jail; for being in a ship is being in a jail, with the chance of being drowned. A man in a jail has more room, better food, and commonly better company. When men come to like a sea-life, they are not fit to live on land.'

The young man now surveyed the doctor as a captain looking to engage the enemy. 'I speak from no great age or experience. I am but a callow midshipman of but one voyage, and I am staying with my father here in Bath until I embark on my next. Already, though, I have decided that there is no life quite like the King's Navy for a man who seeks both adventure and advancement. I give thanks that I have not been in gaol, but I cannot conceive of a life without a horizon to scan and prizes to win. In fact, it would be perfection itself if not for the grievous sea sickness that afflicts me. However, I am assured that the treatment here has now banished it, even if I should never want to drink so much water again. I was advised that adding salt would make it especially efficacious in my case, but it was powerfully not to my taste.'

Mr Barber approached with a brandy, which the midshipman seized with relish. 'Brandy, on the other hand,' he said, taking an enthusiastic swig, 'I might happily drown in.'

The doctor was impressed: 'Well spoken, Sir. I might not agree with you, but I admire your spirit!'

Boswell was impressed: 'Our shores will be the safer with you beyond them, Sir!' Mr Barber was at attention. Mr Bennet fancied he could hear 'Hearts of Oak' issuing up from the Avon and the Severn and the high seas. Boswell continued fawning: 'Could we have the honour and pleasure of knowing whose company is bestowed upon us?'

The young man took another draught. 'Horatio Nelson, midshipman, and, depending on God, the French and my stomach, future Lieutenant, Captain and Admiral of the Fleet.' All of the party except Mr Barber concealed smiles at this.

The doctor, sensing an audience for his opinions fresh in every way, beckoned him: 'Won't you join us, Sir?'

'An honour, Sir, but a rough sailor is hardly fit for such distinguished a company.' His emphasis on 'fit' was lost on no one. 'Besides, this is my last night before I leave to take sail for an expedition to the Arctic. My captain intends to find the North East Passage and I have a fancy to capture one of the white bears they have up there. So tonight I shall have one last Bath sally. Should anyone care to accompany me?'

'Not I, Mr Nelson,' said the doctor. 'I am too old for such things. I do not dance, I am deaf and at these public assemblies I cannot hear myself speak, which is an insufferable loss.' There was, of course, beneath the bombast, an amused side to the doctor, and one which he feared Boswell's art might not be quite up to contriving. 'I shall go to my friends the Thrales. I am in thrall to the Thrales, both Master and Mistress. She beguilingly belies her daintiness, and quite often corrects me, which I find I enjoy.' The doctor was almost twinkling. 'I am in a light mood. It must be,' he said, nodding to the sailor, 'the Nelson touch! Come, Mr Barber. Boswell?'

'I'll join you presently, Doctor. I have a few matters which demand my attention. Perhaps I might walk with you a little, Midshipman?'

Nelson assented, as did Mr Bennet, who was also feeling filliped by the energy and verve of the youth. The three left Walcot Street and began to walk up to the new Assembly Rooms. Darkness had now fallen and a Bath breeze had come up, causing the varied passers-by to clutch at hats and check apparel. 'Broadsiding weather,' piped young Nelson with relish. As they passed an alleyway off Bartlett Street, they heard a woman cry.

'That's Bath, I fancy, Sirs,' said Boswell with a smile whose intention to confide and indulge was marred by its execution and achieved more of a leer.

'Let us see if we can lend assistance,' said the midshipman, eager for any action. Mr Bennet was game to follow, and did; it was a little time before he noticed that Boswell had not set the same course, and was nowhere to be seen.

In the alley, Nelson and Mr Bennet found themselves confronting two men and a woman. One of the men, scarred, and with a pronounced squint, was dressed in a shabby vagabond way. The other was as extraordinary a sight as Mr Bennet had encountered since he had left Longbourn, not excepting the doctor. He was a tall fellow, handsome, but that was the least of it. He was a wearing a coat of pea green velvet, a blue satin waistcoat with silver trimmings, the palest buckskin breeches with eight coloured ribbons hanging from each knee, scarlet stockings, and silver-buckled shoes. He was also pointing a pistol at a young woman in languid fashion while his companion menaced her with an evil-looking cudgel which by its state was clearly a veteran of many a horrible assault.

The young woman was quite a beauty, dark-eyed and finely fashioned. Although backed up against the alley wall, she seemed splendidly unperturbed, maintaining an unstaunchable torrent of reproach and general commentary on the failings of Bath: 'How dare you, Sirs? How dare you!? A young lady has but to step out from the dance for some welcome cooling air – Bath is so stuffy! – when she is manhandled into a most unsuitable alley for one of her standing – I am related, admittedly at a distance in some cases, to many of the finest families in Essex, including the Dyers of Billericay – Mr Dyer is the younger son of the younger son of the Earl of Walford, and must be worth at least £4,000 a year and you should know I am come directly from two dances with his friend, Mr Winstone, who is unmarried and has a comparable income, although Canvey is smaller than one might wish. As it happens, I am yet to be spoken for, but pray do not assume this makes me suitable prey for the likes of you, a scented popinjay and his noisome confederate. Yes, you, Mr Squint. It means that you smell. And stop waving your unspeakable object at me, Sir!'

Mr Bennet, taking this all in, found himself to his amazement and delight the victim of that most desirable and figurative of cudgels, that of Desire. To him the young woman seemed the perfected union of beauty and spirit, with a lively view of the proprieties and cost of living thrown in. He was, truly, another man smitten in Love and Bath.

While he stood there with an unusually foolish expression on his face, the midshipman opted for action. With a fierce, if shrill, cry, he rushed at the two rogues, coming at them down the alley from behind and the side. They turned swiftly, and the dandy neatly flipped the small onrushing youth into the arms of the vagabond, shouting to his grubby accomplice, 'Hold him fast, Mr Gove!'

Using the midshipman's assault as a distraction, the young woman had the presence of mind to slip away from the wall, but not before delivering the dandy a sharp kick to the shin. 'Wearing pea green in September, indeed!' The dandy attempted to arrest her flight, but succeeded only in ripping the front of her gown, revealing the most comely embonpoint, heaving with the excitement and effort of her escape. If Mr Bennet was transfixed before, he was dumbfounded now; but he collected himself manfully and gestured to her to shelter behind him. He then took off his coat and hat and handed them to her over his shoulder with an admirable flourish, commenting with as much insouciance as he could muster, 'Madam, I beg you to allow my coat and hat to protect your modesty and repute. The coat is a poor thing, but at least it is not pea green.' The young woman grasped the garment gratefully, surveying Mr Bennet with a delightful upward glance that would have enslaved if that had not already been accomplished, saying, 'Thank you, Sir. A gentleman at last!'

'Have a care with those insolences, Sir and Madam,' said the dandy, who had paused to address them while his accomplice struggled to cope with the angry midshipman. He pointed to his knee ribbons with a graceful sweep of the hand not holding his pistol and announced, 'You have the honour to be addressed by none other than Sixteen-String Jack, the greatest gentleman of the road in England!'

'Gentleman! Of the road!' responded the young woman. 'You're in an alley! Some gentleman, I should say! And with that blackguard and his... his... filthy appendage! And now he is attacking a young boy!'

'My compliments, Madam!' shouted Nelson before sinking his teeth into the hand of Mr Gove's which held the cudgel. Mr Gove cursed in a most ungentlemanly manner, dropped the cudgel, but still held hard to the struggling boy.

'Madam, you do my companion a gross disservice,' said Sixteen-String Jack. 'It is his valet's day off and his cudgel is a family heirloom.'

Jack was now pointing his pistol full at Mr Bennet; it was a mark of that gentleman's newly discovered ardour that his heart filled with yet more admiration for the feisty girl behind him, without a care for his own exposed position between her and Jack. 'You, Sir,' he told Jack, 'are no gentleman of a kind that I recognise. You have failed to remove your hat and that pistol has never seen the inside of the workshop of James Barbar, the only gunsmith that I would trouble.'

Jack, in no whit flustered, replied, 'Ah, I see some sense in the gentleman's approach. You note I honour you with that term, although you permitted young Neptune here to intervene for the lady's honour while you were gawping at her charms. This pistol is, in fact, the work of William Turvey of Shoe Lane, and he would not take kindly to a disparagement in favour of Mr Barbar, whose father, I understand, was French.'

'That doesn't look like a Turvey to me. Let me have a look at it.'

'Ha! A saucy effort, Sir! As if I would oblige you in that! I am not some tyro brigand: I am Sixteen-String Jack Rann, the legend of the highways and most byways, too, between Bath, London and beyond, the fear of all men and the hope of every pretty pair of eyes with spirit to be found along them!'

Here Jack winked at the girl, who shook her fist at him, took off one of her pumps and hurled it at him over Mr Bennet's shoulder, shouting, 'And, Sir, there is another where this came from, even though they were a fine price and seemed much to impress Mr Winstone.'

Jack easily dodged the flying slipper. 'As I say, spirit. But I don't want your shoes, Madam, I want your necklace. Please throw that at me instead, before Mr Gove and I become impatient.'

Mr Gove, still tussling with the midshipman, made a guttural noise which suggested urgent assent.

'And you, Sir, that fine fob, your ring, and any money you might have about you.'

'Sir, I have no intention of following any such instruction, and I will not allow the lady to do so, either. I would now advance to give you a good thrashing even though you are hiding in a most ungentlemanly fashion behind a firearm. But I see there is no need, as there is a friend of mine behind you.'

Jack laughed. These incidents, as we have seen, took place some time ago, but even so. 'Do you hear that, Mr Gove? Would you really conceive of me falling for that old pretence? Forgive me, I will doff my hat and you will place your trinkets and coinage in it.'

So saying, Jack swept off his hat, and was immediately felled by Mr Barber, who had indeed come up behind the two rogues. Mr Gove took this as his cue to sprint off up the alley, helped on his way by a nimble kick up his posterior arrangements from the midshipman, who was seething at the indignity allowed by his slightness of stature, and cursing the ban on carrying swords in Bath imposed some years before by Beau Nash.

Jack was now sitting up and ruefully rubbing that part of the back of his head where he had been smitten by Mr Barber with an inscribed volume of the abridged version of the doctor's dictionary. 'And be thankful,' Mr Barber told him sternly, 'that it was not an unabridged volume, as they weigh twenty-one pounds.'

Mr Bennet and the young woman, who had introduced herself as Miss Jane Gardiner, were engaged in a conversation that was not so important as the looks they were exchanging, the nature of which I will leave to the reader's discretion, providing that he or she has ever been in love. (He or she might also be wondering exactly why Mr Barber was carrying a dictionary; I would only mention that Mr Barber was a deeply studious man, and that a servant's devotion to a master can find unusual expression, and is difficult to define.)

At this point, a familiar voice rang out from the end of the alley where Mr Gove had lately speedily exited and whence Mr Barber had earlier made his stealthy way. 'Ah, there you are! Well done, Barber!'

The doctor approached, out of breath, but not that easily silenced. 'Young lady, Mr Nelson, Mr Bennet,' he declared, between sighs, vigorously rubbing his fingers up his forehead and under his wig to allow some ventilation, 'Ill and well met! We were on our way up George Street to the Thrales when we heard the altercation.'

After regaining a little more of his fugitive breath, the doctor confirmed that he had not come across the fleeing Mr Gove, but this was not surprising, as there were even more nooks and crannies availing concealment in old Bath than there are today. Leaning heavily against the wall, he then turned his attention to the recumbent highwayman: 'You, Sir, with the strings: are you aware that robbing a woman is the last refuge of the scoundrel?'

Mr Barber smiled and muttered, 'Bless us, that one again. These scoundrels are certainly busy. That must be at least fifteen last refuges, including patriotism, cucumber and Glasgow.'

Jack smiled too from his sedentary position. 'That's very good, Doctor. I do so agree that robbing a woman is not the mark of a gallant, but times are rather hard.'

'Doctor!? You know me?'

'Everyone knows Dr Johnson. I myself have been deeply impressed by your dictionary,' responded Jack, rubbing the back of his head again.

'That's a pretty sally, sir! Are you always this sharp?'

'Depend upon it, Doctor, when a man knows he might be hanged, it concentrates his mind wonderfully.'

This brisk exchange was now interrupted by a shout from Boswell, who had appeared from the opposite direction. All heads turned. The biographer was admirably unsheepish about his sudden absence, if a little dishevelled, particularly about his lower portion, and elusive as to its explanation. Jack, ever alert to opportunity, seized his moment to escape; being Jack, he was unable to resist turning at the end of the alley to bid adieu: 'Farewell, my lady, Doctor, gentlemen, feisty youth and violent book-lover. I trust we will have the pleasure of meeting again, with a happier result for the great Sixteen-String Jack!'

'And I trust you, Sir, will be truly concentrated!' cried Nelson. Miss Gardiner accompanied this with a vigorous shake of her pretty fist, while Mr Barber took a relaxed view on any possible pursuit. With a mocking bow, doff of the hat and playful wince, Jack was gone. The doctor and Boswell determined to continue to the Thrales with Mr Barber; Mr Bennet had, of course, volunteered to escort Miss Gardiner, now much and bravely recovered, back to her family. But, being Mr Bennet, he had some advice for Nelson before they parted: 'Bravely done, my young friend. But I noticed that when you took on those two rogues, you attacked across them, rather in a manner of a ship of a line readying for a broadside. Might not a direct attack have been preferable, to split them and prevent each from aiding the other?'

The midshipman had his private thoughts about this piece of advice from a Chippendale admiral, as he had about Jack's finery, to which he found himself much attracted. A hero, he thought, especially a small one, has to be seen and to advertise himself. Gold braid and medals were on his mind as he walked back to his quarters after deciding he had undergone sufficient exertions before the morrow. Other matters were on Mr Bennet's. As he walked Miss Gardiner back to the Assembly Rooms, she gave a sudden (and to him) delightful start, and cried, 'Why, I had not noticed! This street is called Bennet Street! Is it your family, Sir? That argues a considerable interest in this fair city.'

Mr Bennet, faced with a quandary of honesty against advantage, commented that his was a large family and turned the conversation to the proximity of Essex to Hertfordshire and his home at Longbourn. Upon hearing that he was the only son of his family, Miss Gardiner became almost skittish. Mr Winstone was to be disappointed. Miss Gardiner was to be Mrs Bennet.

*

ALL THAT HAD BEEN LONG AGO. AS IS WELL KNOWN, Mr Bennet did indeed inherit Longbourn, but could pass it on only to male heirs, of which he had none. This was of great concern to Mrs Bennet, but Mr Bennet was generally more sanguine, particularly as his own demise would be the occasion of this disaster. And he was, despite appearance, fond of his five daughters. His admiration for the virtues and vivacity of the elder two, Jane and Elizabeth, was matched by the entertainment he derived from the foibles and follies of Mary, Lydia and Kitty. True, he did wish for them all to be married, but that was principally because it might persuade Mrs Bennet to seek out another choice for conversation.

No, if Mr Bennet was at all disappointed, it was of a nature mentioned earlier, that of unfulfilment, a condition hardly to be improved by the subsequent careers of his companions that night long ago. Even Sixteen-String Jack had received his moment of high fame, dressed much as in Bath and mocking the gibbet at Tyburn with a little jig before dancing the longer fatal one wished for him by Viscount Nelson. That Mr Bennet was at least still living cut little consolation.

This discontent came to a high peak during the family's third week in Bath. Mr Bennet had so far contrived to escape most engagements and excursions, but the previous night he had finally been prevailed upon by Mrs Bennet to accompany them to the dance at the Assembly Rooms, where he had been subjected to an unending commentary from his wife about the Duke of This and The Countess of That and Sir The Other and every other person present, their distinguished lineage, eligible children and income down to the nearest rounded figure. None of them excited the slightest envy in Mr Bennet: where was the daring, the unconventional and the danger? A plan began to form.

The next day he retired as usual to his library room after lunch. But on this occasion he underlined his demand for privacy by leaving a note attached to the door which read: 'ENTRY FORBIDDEN under any circumstance inferior to the death of the King. This includes communications of requests to seek hand in marriage (Jane), communications of sound advice (Elizabeth), communications of fascinating facts such as the Derbyshire coalfield annual production figures (Mary), requests to run off with subalterns (Lydia) and requests to buy hats (Kitty). Yes, this also includes you, dear Mrs Bennet. In brief, KEEP OUT!'

And so it was that, after an hour or so, Mr Bennet opened fully a sash window and with surprising agility effected an exit from the house through the back yard and into the alley behind it. With a broad smile not generally associated with him, he began a leisurely and enjoyable tour of the Bath booksellers, particularly enjoying Mr Leake's, until that worthy attempted to press a copy of Boswell's *Life of Johnson* on him. His next call, inevitably, was to the Pelican Inn, where, sadly, fresh disappointment awaited: not only were there stolid and dull parties at every table, but even its name had been changed, to The Three Cups. Discovering the mine hoste by looking out the most doleful man present, he enquired of that individual, who was sighing repeatedly over a newspaper, where might be found lively stimulation of the wits by company of the same turn. 'Next coach to London leaves from The White Hart at three o'clock,' replied the man, scarcely lifting his eyes from the print.

Mr Bennet was confirmed in his opinion that Bath was not what it was; but raised a smile from the only man present likely to appreciate it, viz, himself, by reflecting that this had always been the case. Evening had now arrived, but, reluctant to return to his home so short of an adventure, he walked on in the direction of the Pump Room. As he neared there, he was disconcerted to discern, not far away, his family, clearly intent on the same destination. Rapidly retracing his steps, he turned into Cheap Street, where, to his further surprise, he found a man beckoning him from the dark entrance to Union Passage.

This man was dressed in a fashion approximate to what was currently acceptable, but there was a thinness, an imitative quality to his coat and hat which argued an unfamiliarity with anything approaching a gentleman's tailor. This did not prevent him adopting a familiar tone with Mr Bennet, however, a tone which also confirmed his position some rungs down on the Ladder of Advancement and Entitlement. In short, he had at some stage made the opposite journey to that suggested by the landlord of the Three Cups, but at less expense.

Staring into Cheap Street while fiddling with some frayed and loose frogging on his coat, he addressed Mr Bennet out of the side of his mouth: 'Now then, Your Lordship, you look a man as enjoys some sport. Won't you follow me?'

Mr Bennet, conscious of the increasing propinquity of his family, and, as we have seen, not unreceptive to some unaccustomed excitement, followed as the man walked up the passage, turned left and entered a house of a plush if faded decoration.

The man turned and smiled at Mr Bennet in what he obviously imagined to be an encouraging and welcoming fashion but whose effect was severely countered by his squint, several scars, a number of missing teeth and the state of those remaining. 'So, Sir,' he enquired, in an insinuating manner. 'What's your fancy?'

'Well, Sir,' rejoined Mr Bennet. 'You spoke of sport. As we are inside, this seems unlikely to be quoits, Hairry My Bossie, Boggle About the Stacks or Bandy Ball. I fear, too, Snapdragon or Blind Man's Buff would be a trifle dull with but the two of us.'

'Hah, very good, my lord! I see we have a regular sportsman with us! As it happens, I am here to tell you that we do from time to time indulge in some indoor games. Some concern cards and some concern what you might call other objects to scrutinise closely and find your luck's in. What's it to be, Your Highness?' The man leered again. Mr Bennet found he was rather enjoying himself.

'Oh, cards, I think. Although I must warn you that I have something of a reputation in Hertfordshire. There are those who even go so far as to warn against engaging with me at any version of the four suits, but particularly Irish Snap.'

'Hah again, Your Worship! You are, if I might make so bold as to coin a phrase, a card! I venture that you will enjoy yourself here, as we have a party about to undertake a game of Faro.'

'Faro! That I do enjoy from time to time. High stakes, I assume?'

'Indeed, Sir. One gentleman ended our last session a good £6000 to his benefit.'

'Well. Small beer for Hertfordshire, but it's the fun of the thing, isn't it?'

'It is, it is, Your Excellency. And I will happily wager the same amount that the party gathered will not be exceeded in pedigree and interest anywhere in the kingdom.'

Although, as usual betraying little, an advantage in playing cards and indeed much else in life, Mr Bennet was in truth beginning to feel quite some alarm and a sudden longing for the view from inside his library. But an adventure was an adventure, so with his customary sangfroid but an elevated heart palpitation, he followed his host, who led him up the next flight of stairs, threw open a door and ushered him into a room containing a large oval table and an assortment of gentlemen in varying degrees of age, station and anticipation. The table was covered in green baize and prepared for Faro; the banker's shoe was in position, and the board with cards attached.

The party surveyed Mr Bennet; Mr Bennet surveyed the party with what he hoped passed for coolness. He knew none of them, although some seemed familiar. One, by the look of him a naval man, had a wooden leg. His host, with some pride, effected introductions:

'Sirs, allow me to introduce Mr Bennet, of Hertfordshire. Mr Bennet, allow me to introduce my Lord Byron, Sir Walter Elliot, Captain Crawley, Mr Silver, Mr Heathcliff, Mr Flashman and Mr Jingle. Captain Crawley will be our banker.'

The gentlemen acknowledged Mr Bennet with differing manner and manners. Lord Byron, oblivious, was staring hard at a blank page of writing paper, muttering to himself abstractedly, as far as Mr Bennet could make out, 'How to start? Yes, but how, how?' Sir Walter failed to take his eyes off Lord Byron. Captain Crawley smiled. Mr Heathcliff glowered. Mr Flashman's expression fell somewhere between. Mr Silver raised his right eyebrow, causing the parrot on his shoulder to shout, 'Steady, my hearties, Pieces of Eight to starboard!' Mr Silver introduced the parrot, without further ado or comment, as Captain Flint. The friendliest member of the party seems to be Mr Jingle: 'Sir. Cards. Capital. Yours. Mine. Soon.' Mr Bennet determined to remove himself from this terrifying company as quickly as possible.

'My lord, gentlemen,' he announced as the company took to the table, 'What a privilege to meet you, and what a pity that I must take leave of you forthwith. It is a cause of much irritation to me, both in my mental and physical capacities, that parrots unfailingly cause me to break out in the most unseemly perturbation of the skin. I have not a moment to lose.'

Mr Silver, seeing a prize about to disappear, graciously offered to remove his companion, or, as he more colourfully phrased it, 'put the mangy old heap of feathers out', but Mr Bennet was firm: 'Thank you, Sir, but unfortunately I fear it is already too late'.

Captain Flint, not at all disconcerted, shouted, 'It's up his sleeve!' eliciting from Mr Heathcliff and Mr Flashman a sudden twitch and a violent start respectively.

'Farewell, gentlemen,' bade Mr Bennet. 'Perhaps we might try again – sans our feathered friend, naturally – another night?'

Captain Flint, apparently without rancour, repeated, 'Another night! Another night!'

As he left the room, Mr Bennet heard Lord Byron exclaim, 'Of course! That's it! That's how she walks in beauty! I'm up and running at last!'

Mr Gove appeared on the stair. 'Going so soon, Your Grace? A tremendous pity, particularly as we are awaiting a young gentleman attached to a large estate in Derbyshire whose dreadful run of luck at the table shows no sign of running out and most likely will not for the foreseeable future.'

He accompanied this with an exaggerated wink that contorted the largest scar on the side of his face, and continued, 'But if you are determined to deprive the table, I know Mrs Crawley would be more than honoured if you were to join her and some of her young lady friends in her quarters.'

He repeated the wink, combining it this time with one of his previous leers. Mr Bennet began to worry that he was indeed allergic to parrots. At this point, the door of the card room was flung open and Captain Crawley shouted, 'Gove! Drink!'

Mr Bennet and Gove looked at each other. 'Tell me, Sir,' said Mr Bennet. 'Were you ever acquainted with the late Mr Sixteen-String Jack?'

'Not I, Your Majesty. I venture to say that such a connection would be as likely as your visiting a house unbecoming to the reputation of a country gentleman and your family somehow becoming aware of it. Good day.'

'In that case, you will not remember an occasion some years ago when Jack and an accomplice were prevented from assaulting a charming young woman by myself and a young midshipman called Nelson.'

'No, I can't say as I do. But I wept when I heard of the admiral's great victory and death. It would have been a privilege to know England's Hero in any circumstances, even to be bitten by him, I should dare to say. Now I must refresh my current masters. Good evening, Sir.'

Mr Bennet emerged from the house and Union Passage and made his way back to Gay Street without further adventure, unless the trifling matter of a split to his breeches climbing in through his library window is taken into account. He blamed this on too many Bath buns; his daughter Jane cheerfully repaired it and Mr Bennet, not for the first time, wondered how he would ever be able to get on without her, or his dear Lizzie, who teased him while Jane sewed. And, as he was in a relieved and mellow mood, he went to far as to extend this wish to his three younger daughters; even Lydia.

He also resolved on no further Bath escapades and

determined that a library life was for him. He imagined himself finally completing one of his projects, a work of clever and delicate humour about his family and its fortunes. And, that night, Mrs Bennet, dear, silly, beautiful Mrs Bennet, rediscovered her gentle hero, rescuer and lover.

Afterword

NONE OF THE EVENTS DESCRIBED IS COMPLETELY *implausible, save the presence of Mr Bennet and his family, and several other fictional characters.*

MR BENNET (his first name not vouchsafed) is for some the true hero of Pride and Prejudice, *the most successful novel of JANE AUSTEN (1775–1817). It has sold over twenty million copies since it was published to scant attention in 1813. The book concerns the fortunes of the Bennet family, and particularly those of the five Bennet daughters, as their excitable but formidable mother, Mrs Bennet, née Jane Gardiner, campaigns to acquire wealthy and well-connected husbands for them, while their father holds to his library until it is too late. Other heroes and villains and lasting attachments do not immediately disclose themselves, but include that of Jane Bennet to Mr Bingley, a wealthy man but lately arrived in the neighbourhood, and Elizabeth Bennet's to both his unfriendly friend, Mr Darcy, of Derbyshire, even wealthier, and a connection of his, Mr Wickham, a charming fellow of uncertain antecedent and most vices, including the gaming tables, where he seems to have had a talent for loss.*

Bath features more or less in all of Jane Austen's novels. She had visited several times before her father, the Reverend George Austen, decided to retire there from his living in Steventon, Hampshire, Jane's hitherto happy home; she and her elder sister, Cassandra, also unmarried, had little choice but to go with him. The family lived in Sydney Place, Green Park Buildings, and, after her father's death, Gay Street. Jane and her sister and mother left for Southampton in 1805 'with happy feelings of escape': she would no doubt have much enjoyed the Austenesque irony of now being invariably and proudly described as its most famous resident.

DR SAMUEL JOHNSON (1709–1784), hero of English letters, was a visitor to Bath on more than one occasion, and stayed at The Pelican. He also visited his friends the Thrales, who also lived in Gay Street. HESTER THRALE (1741–1821), married to the wealthy London brewer, Samuel Thrale, was a particular friend of the doctor; indeed, a recent book has alleged that he and Mrs Thrale enjoyed private relations of a disciplinary nature. Much of the doctor's dialogue is authentic. He was indeed in the habit of collecting orange peel, which has been a subject of much speculation as he refused to tell Boswell why. Mr Bennet would doubtless have been much entertained to learn later that the doctor, despite his declared affection for port, claret, brandy, and of course a 'hardened and shameless' tea drinker, suggested the Greek phrase that decorates the new Pump Room's pediment and declares that 'Water is best'.

JAMES BOSWELL (1740–1795), lawyer, laird, lecher and possibly the world's most famous biographer, accompanied his subject on his visits and stinted not in satisfying his passions while so engaged.

FRANCIS BARBER (1742/3–1801) was Dr Johnson's Jamaican manservant, a slave freed and educated by Johnson, a fierce opponent of slavery. He also had a spell in the navy, to which Johnson was almost as opposed; the doctor succeeded in having him released from service, not entirely willingly, through the intercession of a remarkable pair, John Wilkes and Tobias Smollett. He returned to serve Johnson and was provided for in his will, provided he moved to Lichfield, the doctor's home town, where he farmed and founded a village school.

A person of colour such as Mr Barber would have been a more familiar sight in Bath, where many families had black servants, and many more owed their wealth and ease to slave plantations in the Caribbean and the Americas. Even Miss Austen's clergyman father had an interest in a plantation in Antigua (there is some discussion about which side Jane stood on, but I think we can be pretty sure). The two great financiers of Georgian Bath, the Duke of Chandos and Sir William Pulteney, were plantation owners in the Caribbean and the Americas. Pulteney's daughter, the Laura of Laura Place, owned estates in Tobago and Dominica. And then there was the very rich and very eccentric William Beckford, whose possessions included work by Rembrandt, Poussin, Claude, Bellini and 3,000 human beings in Jamaica. Apparently seeing no contradiction between his aesthetic sensitivities and the source that supported them, he wasted most of it on follies, including Beckford's Tower, which still looms over Bath as an apt symbol of the dangers of too much money and too little conscience. It cannot be denied, though, that his mighty pink granite sarcophagus in the small cemetery specially commissioned to take it should be seen.

Bath did atone a little for its part in slavery by welcoming the great reformer, WILLIAM WILBERFORCE, and one of the writers of the day, HANNAH MORE, his fellow philanthropist and abolitionist. Mrs More lived in Bath and Wilberforce spent much time in the city, for his health, and his heart: he met his wife-to-be, Barbara Spooner in Bath, and married her here. It is more or less ironic that both Wilberforce and More lived for a time in Great Pulteney Street. WILLIAM PITT, Wilberforce's friend, Prime Minister and anti-slavery prime mover, was a frequent visitor to Bath for his health, as was his father, fellow gout-sufferer and prime ministerial predecessor, WILLIAM PITT THE ELDER, who was MP for Bath from 1757 to 1766. Mr Barber's descendants still farm in the Lichfield area.

Vice Admiral HORATIO NELSON, 1st Viscount Nelson, 1st Duke of Bronté, (1758–1805), England's Hero, has many Bath connections. His father, the Reverend Edward Nelson, visited Bath annually for his health after the death of his wife, Catherine, when Horatio was nine. Two of his sisters worked for a time as milliners at Messrs Walters of Milsom Street. There is no definitive record of a visit by the young Nelson until 1781, when he had treatment for a tropical disease, but it seems unlikely it was his first. There is a beguiling story that the future Lady Hamilton was working as a maid across the street from where he was convalescing in 1781, but it wants fact. Nelson went to sea in 1771 at the age of thirteen; by the time he was fifteen he had crossed the Atlantic twice and discovered, among much else, a propensity to sea sickness. In 1773, he got wind of an expedition to find a North East Passage to India and secured a berth as coxswain on the splendidly named HMS Carcass. The attempt was foiled by ice. While the ship was trapped, Nelson decided to bag a polar bear skin for his father. His musket misfired in the attempt; never, as we have seen, backwards at coming forwards, Nelson launched a frontal attack with the butt of his weapon. Fortunately for him and the future of his nation, the ice began to crack and separated the combatants before either came to harm.

JACK RANN (1750–1774), Sixteen-String Jack, was a highwayman of great fame. He was born near Bath and became an early example of celebrity, insisting on telling his victims exactly who he was, somewhat redundantly given his uniquely stylish dress. He was accustomed to being acclaimed during his public appearances in satin blue and silver. It was a lifestyle incompatible with his calling, and his end at Tyburn at the age of only twenty-four was sadly inevitable. As it happens, the doctor was an admirer: 'Yes, Sir, Sixteen-String Jack towered above the common mark.'

LORD BYRON (1788–1824) requires little elucidation. His daughter, Allegra, by Claire Clairmont, Mary Shelley's step-sister, was born in Bath. MARY SHELLEY wrote most of Frankenstein while living in the city.

Sir Walter Elliot is the deliciously impossible snob in Miss Austen's Persuasion, *forced by his incautious spending to move from the ancestral home at Kellynch to a rented house in Camden Place.*

Captain RAWDON CRAWLEY fancies himself rogueish and resourceful but is really the long-suffering and not very bright husband of the inimitable Becky Sharp, the entrancingly ill-behaved heroine of Thackeray's Vanity Fair, *cuckolder and con on the make.*

JOHN SILVER is Stevenson's great anti-hero, cook, rascal and fugitive from Treasure Island *and most likely to have turned up later in Bath, renowned at this time for its private card games and callow sprigs and scions ripe for the fleecing.*

Mr HEATHCLIFF, you will recall, was the dangerous fellow created by Miss E Brontë.

Mr FLASHMAN, you will also recall, was the villain of Tom Brown's Schooldays *created by Thomas Hughes and given a magnificently entertaining afterlife by George MacDonald Fraser. This is his father, Henry Buckley Flashman, a man with an even laxer approach to the proprieties, if that is possible.*

Mr ALFRED JINGLE, rogue of them all, must have served his time in Bath before emerging gloriously in Mr Dickens' Pickwick Papers.

It's also not inconceivable that Bennett Street was the inspiration for the name of the family in Pride and Prejudice, *particularly as it was written around the time of Miss Austen's first visit to Bath; and was originally spelt with only one 't', as in the Bennet family of Widcombe*

Manor, for whom it is named. Where once was the Three Cups and the Pelican now stands the Bath Hilton, noted by Pevsner as 'the most reviled building in Bath,' and high mark of the clumsy redevelopment last century. It doesn't seem to remember the doctor, either. In less prudish times, Union Passage was known as Cock's Lane.

Searchers after more Austen will be well served by a visit to the Jane Austen Centre in Gay Street, just along from her former lodgings. There are guided tours; mine was conducted by a gentleman in the naval uniform of Jane's day: 'I'm Captain Wentworth,' he told us. 'It's a thing, just go with it.' By way of confirmation he was also wearing a name badge that read 'Captain Wentworth'. The Captain, he of the stout heart that won the silly Sir Walter Elliot's daughter Anne in Persuasion, gave us an excellent lecture on the Austen family and then led us to the informative exhibition. In a previous life, he said, he had been a bookseller. Afterwards, on the top floor, there was a choice of refreshment which included Tea with Mr Darcy and Mrs Bennet's Cake of the Day. And do have a word with the present Mr Bennet, who is stood outside most days, rain or shine ('I've been out here in a blizzard. You don't get enough dedicated people today'). In his previous life, he was the Pumper in the Pump Room. He is formidably informed, full of interesting speculations, but not overwhelmed by Austen partiality: although Pride and Prejudice is indeed his favourite book, he has a cavil: Jane's punctuation: 'Had the Georgians heard of full stops? Methinks not.'

See:

> *The Jane Austen Centre, 40 Gay Street, BA1 2NT (janeausten.co.uk).*
>
> *The Assembly Rooms, Bennett Street, BA1 2QH (nationaltrust.org.uk).*
>
> *The Fashion Museum, The Assembly Rooms (fashionmuseum.co.uk).*
>
> *Beckford's Tower and Museum, Lansdown Rd, Bath BA1 9BH (beckfordstower.org.uk).*
>
> *Nelson, while a young captain, stayed at 2, Pierrepont Street, BA1 1LB.*

Read:

> Pride and Prejudice, *by Jane Austen, 1813.*
>
> Persuasion, *by Jane Austen, 1817.*
>
> The Pickwick Papers, *by Charles Dickens, 1837.*
>
> Vanity Fair, *by William Makepeace Thackeray, 1847.*
>
> Wuthering Heights, *by Emily Bronte, 1847.*
>
> Treasure Island, *by RL Stevenson, 1883.*
>
> Nelson and Bath, *by Louis Hodgkin, 2004.*
>
> Jack, Stories of Britain's Favourite Name, *by Charles Nevin, 2008.*

Bladud Takes Flight

I TOLD HIM HE WAS A FOOL EVEN TO THINK OF IT AT his age. But you know how it is with kings, or perhaps, luckily and unluckily, you don't. They like advice because it makes them feel important but they don't take it because that would make them feel less important. So I was a fool to tell him, but that is what I am: court jester to King Bladud, eighth in descent from Brutus the Trojan, first ruler of this chilly island, to which he lent his name after arriving here as part of the fallout from that heroic but complicated affair just east of the Aegean.

It's not everyone's idea of a good job, fooling. Ridiculous outfit, complicated wordplay, unsocial hours and a high risk of sudden death if your audience decides that wasn't very funny. Seven kings and one queen since Brutus; twenty-three fools. Not much competition for the job, unsurprisingly. Still, I'm young and it seemed preferable to harrowing, scratching or eking. Youngest sons do of course have a traditional path into druidry, but I'm allergic to mistletoe, not to mention blood sacrifice and screams.

And Bladud is wonderful. His last fool, Dodd, who could go on a bit, died of old age, which was not the experience of the others with other kings. Bladud's father, Rud Hud Hudibras, was as grumpy as he sounds. Not like Bladud. He's an old man now, but an old man of the sort that cherishes curiosity and smiles on youth without envy. Who else, for example, would have decided to fly at the age of sixty-eight? Fly!

I asked him why, breaking off from what I hoped was a bit of artfully artless capering by the side of his great bath, magnificently colonnaded and gently steaming beneath its stupendously pitched roof. 'Stop jerking about, boy,' he said. 'And you need to do a lot more pig's bladder work. Shake it as though you mean it. Like all kings, I crave undying, undimmed fame. Flying will really clinch it. I've studied the matter and it's really not that difficult. A pair of wings cunningly constructed from yew and feathers, strap them on, jump from a high point, flap and fly!'

'There are sires who soar and there are sires who are sore from a soar with a flaw, methinks, Sire. Have you heard of Icarus?'

'Heard of him? I used to know the fellow when I was living in Athens. Talked a good game, but I was never convinced by his commitment, to be honest. That's the trouble with the Greeks as a whole, if you ask me. Not willing to do the hard slog, all fancy tricks and short cuts like that unsporting bit with the wooden horse that did for my forebears. And if they're not doing that, they're sitting around moodily asking each other why they're there. I told Icarus he'd have trouble from the sun with that wax. And that he'd better placate Apollo before take-off. Took not a blind bit of notice. That's why I'm building a flyplace dedicated to Apollo on top of Solsbury Hill and using straps and yew, not wax.'

I decided to try another tack. 'But, Sire, you have already achieved undying fame! What better bid than Bath?! The known world's hottest city! Discovered by you, founded by you, built by you, Nuncle!' (I call him Nuncle because he's not my uncle, if you follow.)

Bladud sank beneath the waters and then re-emerged. I passed him his britannicals shampoo and he lathered up. Others might have looked ridiculous, but Bladud had the dignity of a stone carving as the suds mingled with his white dreadlocks. 'Yes, that's all very well, but the fame that endures comes from brave deeds and legendary exploits. I am descended from the mighty Aeneas, legendary champion of Troy and son of Aphrodite. His son was Brutus, who has this entire country named after him. They can't even be bothered to name Bath after me. Not famous enough, you see. I'm regarded at best as some sort of bath house proprietor. Even my founding myth has turned out badly. Too much pig. A fine creature, your pig, but not exactly dashing and heroic. Rome has wolves, you know. Now if the story had involved a wolf, or better, a lion or a bear, or, even better, both, rather than some semi-scrofulous porkers, that would have been different. Flying pigs might have done it, possibly.'

Bladud was now blowing bubbles from his soap in a faraway fashion. I decided on a brisker approach. 'What about a spot of war, Sire? As you say, it's always good for building a reputation. That lot over the Channel are usually up for a scrap.'

'War is very messy. I've never been very keen on gore and shouting and waving things around. There's all the camping, too. Flying will be so clean, and liberating, up there in the sky, flapping and floating, twisting this way and that, making lazy circles in the sky, laughing out loud at the sheer fun and joy of it. And if it goes wrong, so be it. At least I'll get to see my beloved Queen Gert. I miss her, Fool.'

You must have begun to see what I was up against. What a wonderful man Bladud was! So unpomped and unprimped, so full of life and spark and love. You must have begun to see why I couldn't bear to risk losing him a day before his time, or why he wouldn't care a sud for mockery from the earth-bound and the doltish.

'Well, then, Nuncle, tell me this: what issue would your issue have with your issue with living?'

'Oh, by Brutus, it's riddle time. I have to say that of all the diversions in the fool's repertoire, the riddle is my least favourite. A lot of effort for not a huge amount of entertainment, in my view.'

'Oh, come on, Sire, have a go!'

'All right, all right. Give me another clue.'

'Who will succeed without trying when you have tried and not succeeded?'

'Eh? No, hold on, it's about issue and succeeding, isn't it? Is it my son Lear?

'He's very worried about you. Worried for you. He doesn't want you to die.'

'Well, well. I'm afraid to say I've lost a bit of interest in family matters now dearest Gertie isn't here to prompt me. But you're right, Lear has been looking a bit miserable lately. I put it down to those ghastly daughters of his.'

'Your beautiful granddaughters, Sire?'

'Oh, really. Regan and Goneril are little monsters and Cordelia is a frightful wet. They'd certainly drive me mad. Will you swear to look after him when I've gone?'

'A fool to care for a king? That's never going to work, as the wise servant said to the senile master who'd decided to fly. We'll probably end up homeless on some blasted heath or other.'

'Even so, I'd like you to try. He never gives anything away, but I don't think he has too many people with his interests at heart, especially since his wife left for Elysium, or more probably Hades, bloody difficult woman at the best of times, no, perhaps that's unfair, very liberal views on parenting all the same. Pigs!'

A large pig arrived at the side of the bath carrying a folded towel on its back. It was followed by three successively smaller pigs bearing the king's crown, sceptre and talcum powder. I averted my eyes, as was traditional, until I heard the king command, 'Trotters Ho!' We then processed, pigs first, leading the king, now wearing the crown and the towel wrapped round his ample waist, sceptre held proudly, to the Royal Wardrobe, where he donned his splendid scarlet towelling robe with ermine-effect edging and matching silken cord.

From there we moved into the Throne Room, with its imposing murals of Bladud and Gert gazing calmly and directly at those assembled, who included Lear, a deputation of druids after a donation, and some local citizenry objecting to plans for a new travel lodge near their hovels. Below the thrones, one now poignantly empty, a flame flickered from the mouth of a recumbent bronze goddess, guarded by two pigs wearing helmets who from time to time stoked the burning black stones said to be eternal. One of the objectors approached the throne, where Bladud had taken his place, and addressed the king: 'Mighty ruler, we were wondering who the flaming statue is meant to be.'

'Ah, yes, glad you asked, that's very interesting,' said Bladud, leaning forward in his usual friendly way. 'The eternal flame honours a number of deities, according to choice. As a Anglo-Trojan, I'm committed to a multicultural society embracing faiths not faith. So it can be Aphrodite, my distinguished eight-times grandmother on my father's side and the inspiration for my discovery of these magical baths; or it could also be [and here Bladud smiled at the druids with the sympathetic smile of one magnanimously tolerating the deluded] a rather shadowy local goddess with the slightly less melodious moniker of "Sul."

Sul's melodiousness was not helped by Bladud's pronunciation, which placed apostrophes around the name as if they were tongs handling a dodgy chop. The druids shifted uneasily, but, conscious of their mission, said nothing, merely sketching an indeterminate finger gesture in front of them as if to ward off evil. I smiled across at Lear, who frowned at me as usual. He had heard as often as I Bladud's private view of Sul: 'Bloody ignorant oak botherers are always inventing completely unconvincing bits of mythology. Sul! I ask you! What an ugly language Brit is; Trojan's far more poetic and expressive. But I'm prepared to tolerate their druidy nonsense if it stops them getting the hump and egging on the locals to rush around in blue, looting and such.'

Bladud asked the objectors to explain their opposition to the new lodgings. The spokesman, a thin man called Monbiot, said the development would flatten lots of hovels and that there was a problem with chariot access to the site. A representative of the builders, a fat man called Psimmon, said the lodgings would provide much-needed bed space for visitors and yes, it was unfortunate that a few peasant homes and some green fields would be lost, but the hovels were ugly and what were fields when progress and an improved resort offer were at stake? Bladud said that the lodgings could go ahead if the fields were spared and all the peasants given improved social housing. Psimmon said he couldn't possibly afford to do that; Bladud suggested he should use the large bonus he had awarded himself in the last financial year. 'Good old Bladud!' cried the locals, retreating backwards and out of the Throne Room at speed while Psimmon followed rather more slowly, head bent over his abacus, thumbs racing.

The druids were looking expectant. They went into one of their usual chanted perorations; I caught only bits of it: 'vital work', 'outreach', 'building a temple with a 200 cubit radius doesn't come cheap'. By now, I was standing next to the king, trying to look as inconspicuous as a fool wearing a surcoat of ochre and cerise and a cap with a bell on the end can. When the druids had finally ended their presentation, I nudged Bladud with the end of my bladder stick, as he had fallen sound asleep. He came to with the aplomb of a practised monarch, pronounced the peroration 'most informative and strikingly atonal' and told Lear to give them a suitable donation. The prince shared out ten britcoins between the druids according to some complicated calculation of his own; they left with the air of charioteers who hadn't been tipped quite enough. Bladud shook his head: 'Lear, my boy, don't divide things up, only leads to trouble.'

Lear looked a touch upset, but then he always looked a touch upset. 'I'm not sure I'd take any advice from a man who thinks he can fly,' he said, tartly.

Bladud smiled. 'Oh, but you should, you should. You'd do much better to go for some excitement rather than sitting around all the time worrying whether people like you. Every king should do something extraordinarily out of the ordinary if he wants to be remembered. To risk a little foolishness for fame: it's what we're for. Think on, dear boy, think on.' Lear left, muttering about what things he was going to do when he had worked out what they were, and some other grumpy heir-to-the-throne stuff that I didn't quite catch. The pigs came to attention, saluted Bladud and marched out.

'Lunchtime,' said Bladud. 'Pigs get very hungry, you know. Remarkable creatures. Highly intelligent and easily trained. Terrible waste to eat them. Did you know that their penises operate like a screw, left-hand thread?'

'That's an image as might catch on, Nuncle. But I thought you blamed pigs for the lack of traction for your founding myth?'

'True, true. But I also have a lot to thank them for. Constant hot water is not to be sniffed at. And I'm partly to blame for the concentration on them in the story because I like them. There was more to it, you know.'

'Such as?'

'No, it was all a long time ago and I have a flight to plan.'

'If you tell me, I'll never ask you again what tricks but doesn't lie, is a joke but isn't funny, and causes pain behind but not in the side.'

'That's an easy one. Your terrible riddles themselves. Done. Sit on the steps and listen. It was after I returned from my grand tour of Athens and Rome. The trip didn't go that well. The Greeks aren't really keen on Trojans of any remove, and Rome was a bit basic. Everyone thought I had a stutter because my father was called Rud Hud Hudibras, and, to put the bronze hat on it, I ate some bad mussels in Boulogne on the way back and got the most terrible rash. Livid blotches everywhere. My father took one look at me and told me to disappear until it cleared up, as a leprous-looking heir was not good for morale (he was fighting one of his interminable civil wars at the time). So from Canterbury – which, as I hope you know, he founded – I took the Highway to the Sun in my chariot with my noble white horse, Trygga, passing by Stonehenge, usual trippers and queue, the light glinting off its great golden dome. Then, as the day wore on into the high-heavy bee-buzz of a summer afternoon, I came to the forests of Mendip, where, by the side of the road, stood, or rather snoozed, oinked and truffled, a herd of the ugliest, scruffiest pigs you have ever seen.

'As I slowed to look at this bedraggled crew, a man stepped into the road, holding up his hand and looking very agitated. He told me he had just heard his wife was very ill and he needed to get back home as quickly as possible. Would I mind his pigs while he borrowed my chariot?'

'Nuncle, I thought I was the fool.'

'Yes, yes, I know, but I was young and he was very convincing. Besides, I reasoned if I had his pigs he would bring the chariot back.'

'Except it turned out they weren't his pigs.'

'How did you know that?'

'Come on, the my-swine-your-chariot scam? One of the oldest hustles in the book!'

'Well, I'd never come across it, obviously. Maybe it wasn't so well known in those days. Anyway, after a few minutes, a beautiful young girl came walking through the forest. She had hair the colour of corn at harvest and eyes the colour of corn in spring. And also cheeks the colour of a ripe pippin, mostly because she wanted to know what I was doing with her pigs. I explained what had happened and she laughed. And laughed. It was a very attractive laugh: I never knew anyone else who could so well mix fun and tease and sympathy in a laugh, but that was Gertie.'

'The Queen was a swineherd?!'

'Don't be such a snob, Fool. This is a pretty mobile society we have here, and I don't just talk chariots. I took you on even though you'd never been anywhere near Eyton or Barrow. When she finally stopped laughing, I was still a bit piqued, despite everything, so I asked her why her pigs were so ugly. She told me they'd been cursed by a horrible old woman after the biggest one had stood on her foot and hadn't apologised. The only way the curse could be lifted was if a handsome prince kissed her.'

'Kissed the old woman or kissed the comely swineherd?'

'I got confused myself and kissed Gert, which was what I wanted very much to do in any case, but she turned into the horrible old woman.'

'I can see why this narrative didn't take off. That's the wrong way round.'

'Quite. The old woman then told me there was another problem. I wasn't a handsome enough prince, what with the after-effects of the mussels and the premature male pattern baldness. And then, as seems contractual with horrible old women, she cackled. To escape, I moved further into the forest, deep, as you might imagine, in thought, following the pigs, who didn't care for the cackle either. Eventually, I came to this place, in its hallowed hollow in the hills, and after much musing, I found myself enveloped in an eerie mist, a strangely warm mist. When I emerged on the other side, the old woman was waiting. "Why, Prince, you're handsome," she said. "And what curls! The pigs aren't bad, either. Kiss me and I will be your princess!"

'I hesitated, as any man would, for she was truly horrible. But a prince, or a jester, is nothing without manners. So, while the pigs politely turned their backs, I did the deed.'

'And?'

'And what?'

'Did the old hag turn into a princess?'

'Use a little imagination, Fool. She did, or else I would not have had those glorious years with Gertie – years, I am proud to confess, that began the instant my dearest one was restored to me. For we continued to kiss, and then took to abandon. And here is the marvellous thing: each time our love came to its shuddering explosive peak, a towering gush of steaming spring came bursting from the ground around us. Three times, Fool – although the second and third were of a diminishing exuberance – and three hot springs, the three hot springs of Bath. The pigs became so excited that they hurled themselves onto the springs and were thrown up and supported on the thrust, bouncing, revolving and giggling. What a day, made even better when Trygga came trotting back minus the scoundrel, who was never heard of again, although there were rumours of a particularly large frog around West Harptree.'

'So pigs did fly, Nuncle?'

'Crack my cheeks, you're right, they did, Fool, and now so will I!'

*

BLADUD THREW HIMSELF WITH TYPICAL VIM AND GUSTO into the Great Aviation, as he liked to call it. A mighty temple, built out of wood for speed, with a flat roof for take-off, rose on top of Solsbury Hill while Bladud and his designer, Musk, worked on the prototype wings and harness. Musk, a forceful fellow, suggested that there should be a test flight with a test pilot, looking meaningfully at me again; Bladud would have nothing of it: 'The first successful flight in history by a fool? Please!' Musk looked meaningfully at me again; I ignored him. Even though I am as cowardly as a wise man, I would have flown to save him; but, being only as brave as a wise man, I did not insist.

The day was what I like to think of as a Bath day, the ochre stone of the baths and temples in glorious contrast to the blue of the clear sky and the deep green of the hills. The air was light and lively as nobles and druids made their way up Solsbury Hill and the rest of the city gathered at its foot. I was doing the warm-up, halfway between them up the hill, my supercilious scrapes to the toffs raising a laugh from those below. I was full of dread, of course, but fools pioneered the show going on, so I led everyone in a rousing version of the great Brit anthem, 'We're on the Woad again'.

Mindful of the fate of Icarus, Musk had decided that the flight should be at noon, when the sun was at its highest. Bladud had slept in the temple (very well, judging by the sounds from his chamber behind the altar). Pigs at attention in blankets embroidered with the king's crest, the golden 'B', for Bath and Bladud, lined the runway. There were light gusts of wind, judged excellent by Musk for flight. When Bladud appeared, dressed in a simple white shift which Musk said would provide uplift, there was a mighty roar from the crowd below; he really was much loved, you know. He then did some stretch and press warm-up exercises before opening his arms in the shape of a cross to allow Musk to strap on the wings. They spanned at least ten cubits but were surprisingly light, as I knew from carrying them up the hill (Bladud had not been amused by my pretence at jumping off with them). A druid approached with mistletoe to tie on, but Bladud waved him away. Musk started the countdown, taken up by all with increasing volume and intensity as number one approached (zero wasn't invented until late in Lear's reign, to explain what he was left with). After the mass shout of 'One!' there was a split second of silence before the king started his run.

He went remarkably well for a sixty-eight-year-old, bounding down the roof and without hesitation launching himself off it. There was a gasp from the crowd as he began to fall, then a cheer as the wind got underneath the wings and he rose back up, followed by a groan then silence and then dreadful cries as he plummeted to earth.

I reached my master first, snarling at the first arrivals from the crowd to keep back; snarling with such hurt and pain that they instantly recoiled. He was clearly going, but he recognised me. 'I've seen Gert,' he said. 'Up there, waiting.' I thought that was the moment, but he rallied and gave me the sweetest, most loving, rueful smile. 'Two fools, eh?' he breathed, and surrendered.

I loved that man. I was in love with that man. But the

first time I got to embrace him, to hug and feel him, was when I picked up his lifeless and broken body. Tears were streaming down my face as I carried him up the hill. No one laughed at the fool. Bladud felt light, for the heft and heart of him had been his soul. I carried him into the temple, and again the look of fierce grief made them hold back, even Lear. I laid my dear friend on the altar, took a brand from a druid and set fire to the building. Some made to put it out, but the power of the fool, the mad disregard for the power of others, checked them. Soon the temple was ablaze and smoke rose into the empty sky.

All manner of people told all manner of tales about that day, about what they saw in that smoke as it climbed. Lear claimed he saw Aphrodite descending to claim her descendant. Others said they saw a vision of Troy, unconquered, with Bladud among Hector and Paris and Aeneas and the other heroes; some made out Bath full of people with big hair and fine clothes and laughter. The druids, naturally, got into some convoluted stuff involving Bladud and flying acorns. But I know what I saw: nothing but my tears.

Afterwards, I went to Lear. I've been with him ever since, although my fearless plain speaking, jokes and riddles (Lear doesn't mind them so much) have done absolutely nothing to prevent our present predicament, sans roof, sans land, sans everything. It's nearly over now, I think. Such raving and insanity and hurt. I don't love Lear like I loved his father, but I have served him for his father's sake. Nearly over now. But I'll be hanged before I watch another king die.

Afterword

Unsurprisingly, given their strangeness and *apparently infinite supply, Bath's hot springs have attracted some splendid theories and explanations over the centuries: the most colourful and predominant involve the city's legendary founder, BLADUD, who makes an assured first appearance in that masterful weaving of legend and lively imagination supported by very few facts,* The History of The Kings of Britain, *by Geoffrey of Monmouth, the twelfth century Welsh cleric and high doyen of historical romance.*

It is a brief cameo: Geoffrey pays far more attention to other (equally unsubstantiated) figures: Bladud's mighty forebear, Brutus the Trojan; Bladud's son, Leir, or Lear, whose sad story so seized Shakespeare; and, of course, Arthur, Guinevere and Merlin, whose enduring fame was thus set in train.

We are told that it was Bladud who 'built the town of Kaerbadum, which is now called Bath, and who constructed the baths there which are so suited to the needs of mortal men'. And little else beyond the extraordinary tale of his fatal attempt at flight. Certainly not the later curious detail that he and his pigs were lepers cured by the waters, which has somehow become a far more leading part of his legend.

One intriguing explanation of both is that their invention was inspired by two of the city's most famous medieval images (both now lost) and both wrongly believed to be Bladud: one, a head mounted in the city walls similar to the mysterious Gorgon's Head which once surmounted the Temple of Sulis Minerva and is now on display at the Roman Baths; the other, a statue of King Edward III which stood above one of the city gates. The Gorgon's Head has wings, hence the concoction of the flying story to explain them, probably to gullible twelfth century tourists; the statue of the king became much eroded and pockmarked, hence the leper story. Tour guides, as I'm sure you have experienced, are often enthusiastic followers of Geoffrey's approach, who probably picked up his story from them. (But not now in Bath, I rush to add, holding my umbrella firmly aloft: the Mayor of Bath's Corps of Honorary Guides has continued imparting impartially, enthusiastically and learnedly since 1934, undeterred by war and weather except in a couple of the most extreme cases.)

I have also tried to take a leaf of vellum out of his exhilarating chronicle as far as I am able. So, while there is no evidence that Lear's Fool was also Bladud's Fool, or, indeed, that either of them, if they existed, actually had a fool, it does make for a good story.

I'm also happy to dismiss fashionable modern doubts that the fool is hanged in the Bard's great gusty tragedy. 'And my poor fool is hanged' (King Lear, *Act Five, Scene Three*), *seems pretty clear to me. But I cannot explain how Aphrodite, Greek goddess of love, Brutus's godly grandmother, somehow became confused with Athena, Greek goddess of wisdom, translated by the Romans into Minerva and conjoined with the local goddess Sul or Sulis to become Bath's double-barrelled and trans-religious patroness, Sulis Minerva. I understand that the Gorgons were associated with Athena Minerva, as it was she who angrily created them, but I'm not clear why the Gorgon's Head was named the Gorgon's Head when the Gorgons were women and this is clearly a man.*

I'm inclined to blame a lot of it, like everything else, on the druids and their irritating habit of not writing anything down. Geoffrey, perhaps wisely, is also silent, as he is on Queen Gert and my theory that she is the source of that splendid Bath and Somerset word, gert, or gurt, meaning great.

You might have noticed, too, my robust approach to the firm belief of John Wood, Bath's great and rather odd architect, outlined earlier, that Bladud was a magus and arch-druid. Charles Dickens, a sometime frequenter of Bath, has his own version of the legend in The Pickwick Papers, *but it's not of his best, even though you still marvel at such a gift. Dickens stayed at The Saracen's Head, time-defying and Tardis-like, shortly before creating the small cheery fellow and his friends. (The Bath episode also features a tall Sedan chairman and a small one, but you will have to take on trust that I came upon mine without the aid of Boz.)*

Gerald places the Temple of Apollo in Trinovantum, or ancient London, but it's hard to believe Bladud would have flown from anywhere else but his own city; there are also tales of a temple to him on the reliably mystical and advantageous launch pad of Solsbury Hill. There have been suggestions, too, that Solsbury Hill is also the site of Arthur's

*legendary battle of Badon, but there's surely not enough
room up there for anything more than a take-off or at best
a skirmish of the sort Bath rugby fans, gathered round their
famous club's pitch on the Recreation Ground, like to refer
to, most incorrectly, as 'just a bit of handbags'.*

*The eternally burning black stones in Bladud's palace
were mentioned by Gerald, and are believed to be the first
written reference to the Somerset coal field.*

*There are two statues of Bladud in Bath. The first has
been sitting in a niche in the King's Bath since the seventeenth
century. Its origins, like most of this story, are uncertain:
the head is older than the body, which joined it at a time
unknown. Beneath it is a plaque from 1699 claiming, without
qualification or hesitation, that Bladud was the founder
of the Baths. The second, of the young Bladud, is of a later
provenance, the work of a busy Bath-based nineteenth century
Italian sculptor, Stefano Pieroni; it once stood on top of a
splendid fountain in Stall Street which rained the warm Bath
waters. But Bath has been a touch fickle with its fountains,
which seems odd for a place famed for its liquid assets. The
fountain in Laura Place, at the end of Pulteney Bridge, only
emerged after residents realised that their planned column,
a rival to Nelson's in Trafalgar Square, might overshadow
their residences just a touch. The Rebecca Fountain, at the
side of the Abbey, deserves to be better acclaimed. It shows
the beautiful bride-to-be of Isaac, chosen for her generous
behaviour to man and camel alike at the well in Abraham's
birthplace; it is not, as you might think, a tribute to Bath's
reputation as a matchmaker, but rather a reminder in 1861
from the Bath Temperance Society, that, as the Greek motto*

on the Pump Room's pediment also proclaims (as we've seen, courtesy of Dr Johnson) 'Water is Best'.

Signore Pieroni's work, itself a re-modelling of an earlier fountain, in turn fell out of favour and ended up in a private garden on Entry Hill. In 1989, it was moved, sans Bladud, to the triangle in Terrace Walk popularly known because of its former subterranean facilities as (forgive them, Mr Nash and Miss Austen) Bog Island. Bladud himself has fared a little better and is now in Parade Gardens, accompanied by a pig, but for how long, who knows.

There is also a less obtrusive eighteenth century relief of the young prince, after the illustration by William Hoare (see earlier), on display in the re-modelled Cross Bath, discrete but now part of the Thermae Bath Spa, which finally emerged in 2006 as the old place's response to the challenges of the new millennium, four years late and £32 million over budget after an exasperating exercise in public-private co-operation involving peeling paint, cracked floors, sacked contractors, the Court of Appeal and the Three Tenors performing an opening concert three years before it finally opened. But only a curmudgeon would deny that the Spa, designed by Nicholas Grimshaw, is a toweringly confident piece of work, marrying old and new, stone and glass, Georgian line and contemporary curve, with a rare success. Within are baths and steam and ice rooms, topped by an open air pool where modern Romans can be observed, seemingly oblivious to the staring plebs below.

Bath has three springs. The King's Spring, indeed the most exuberant, feeds the Roman Baths. The Cross Spring, as you might guess, feeds the Cross Bath. The Hetling Spring, named after the early eighteenth century German family who built their Pump Room on it, now feeds the Bath Thermae Spa and the new, private Gainsborough Bath Spa.

The water arrives from thousands of feet below the Mendips at a temperature of at least 45°C and at a rate of a quarter of a million gallons of water a day, channelling the result of rain that fell 6,000 years ago. How could there not be magic here?

See:

> *The Roman Baths and Grand Pump Room, Abbey Church Yard, BA1 1LY (romanbaths.co.uk).*
> *Thermae Bath Spa, The Hetling Pump Room, Hot Bath Street, BA1 1SJ (thermaebathspa.com).*
> *Gainsborough Bath Spa, Beau St, BA1 1QU (thegainsboroughbathspa.co.uk).*
> *Parade Gardens, Grand Parade, Bath, BA2 4DF (visitbath.co.uk).*
> *Little Solsbury Hill, Batheaston, ST768 679 (nationaltrust.org.uk).*
> *The Mayor of Bath's Corps of Honorary Guides (bathguides.org.uk).*
> *The Saracen's Head, 42 Broad St, BA1 5LP (greeneking-pubs.co.uk).*

Read:

> The History of the Kings of Britain, *by Geoffrey of Monmouth, c.1130.*
> Bladud of Bath: The Archaeology of a Legend, *by John Clark ,1994.*

Curses

SHE WAS DEAD NOT LONG AFTER, OF COURSE. DEATH follows the brooch as surely as it follows life, but quickly. She was quite lucky, really; she rushed out after the brooch when it somehow came unclasped and bounced off the pavement into London Road and the path of a rapidly oncoming mail order delivery van. Neither she nor the driver, a conscientious Pole, stood a chance of avoiding her end; but it was instant, unlike many of the others. The people who rushed to help recoiled from the look on her face; of course they did.

Such a beautiful brooch; so admired throughout its life, which has been long. How long, nobody knows but me. Bronze, certainly. Do you remember it featured when the *Antiques Roadshow* came to Bath? It was much liked by the expert, young fellow, floppy hair, nervous, even though he had it hopelessly wrong. He thought it was Egyptian, thirtieth dynasty or so, just before Alexander arrived and everything changed. The woman who had brought it was charming, vivacious, interested, good television. What was its history, the expert wanted to know: had it been in the family long? Oh, no, she said, she had found it by mistake on eBay when she was really looking for some bronzer for her holiday in Lanzarote. Everybody laughed. Surprising how little these things are worth, he said, but he had to give a value, how much had she paid for it? She blushed fetchingly and said it had been about £75. He said that sadly it wouldn't be much more now.

What is the curious creature that so cleverly forms the brooch? The snake that seems to be devouring itself, its tail in its mouth? That is the Ouroboros, an ancient and much travelled symbol. The accepted view is that it originated in Egypt, which is what deceived the young expert. Most people say that the tail disappearing into the mouth is about the Circle of Life. The alchemists were keen on it. If you should go to the Circus you will see it among the symbols in the frieze designed by its architect, John Wood, assiduous devourer of the occult and arcane.

But there is much more to the Ouroboros. How could there not be when it shows a creature sustaining itself by feeding itself to itself? Jung, in his hazy way, saw it: for him it represented the struggle between the conscious and the unconscious. Freud saw the snake, like everything else, as sexual. It certainly speaks to the Christian unconscious, haunted by the serpent.

Make of this what you will. I will tell you that it is really about the futility of existence and humanity's curious urge to destroy itself. Circle of Death would be better.

Not an immediately attractive ontology, although it persists among certain death cults which still practise human sacrifice of the self-explosive kind. The druids were quite early adopters; that is where this brooch comes from, with history, before it re-surfaced in the Romano-British era, here. It belonged to Totia, daughter of Austus, the wine merchant. She had it from her slave, Cambria. It was all Cambria had left from her home; she had taken it from her dying mother during a punitive raid by Quintus Parvus Britannicus, the Governor of Britannia Superior, who had quartered himself at Aquae Sulis as he found the hot spring remarkably easing for his uncomfortable *magnus digitus* (big toe; gout). She had kept the brooch well concealed until the sad day she showed it to Totia, who immediately demanded it. I could not say that Totia was a kind and gentle mistress. She was spoilt on the proceeds of whichever god you think is to be thanked for wine. She was also about to be married to Quintus's younger son, Secundus, a callow young man who had suffered the misfortune of inheriting his father's looks and had neither talent nor discernment, or else he would not have been marrying Totia.

Totia wanted the brooch for a toga clasp even though she had many others. Cambria had no choice but to hand it over. Totia thought it would be just the thing to wear for her toga and hen party at the baths. It was a most luxurious affair – the Great Bath had been hired exclusively – distinguished by large amounts of Gallic wine (none of the Britannic for Totia) and the singularly unattractive laugh of the hostess, slightly less melodious than a fretful peahen. When the bathed beauties and the less so eventually arose from the bath to be towelled and dressed, Totia discovered the brooch was missing (it was followed immediately after Totia's shriek by Cambria, who knew she would be held responsible).

Some may be surprised that I have no wish to dwell on unpleasantness, but nevertheless we will not tarry over the subsequent events which saw a distrait (and, to be honest, tipsy as a Pict) Totia stagger and stumble in the Temple Courtyard, causing her to let go her grip on her broochless toga and thus revealing herself to Quintus Parvus Britannicus, who had chosen that moment to arrive for treatment of his pulsating pedal extremity. The union with his son was cancelled forthwith.

As I say, Totia was not a kind and gentle person. She did not take this upset in her fortunes well. Her search for vengeance and consolation took a turn familiar to the people of Bath at that time: a curse tablet. These were bitterly inscribed pieces of Mendip lead mixed with Cornish tin thrown into the Sacred Spring and calling on the great goddess Sul, patroness of the Spring and its Baths, to punish the thieves of cherished possessions, often taken while their owners were bathing. Totia had made tablets on numerous occasions, delighting herself with the ingenuity of the punishments she demanded – turning the thief's hands to semi-congealed small squirming serpents and turning his or her brain to wax with a convenient taper issuing from the right ear close to a candle was a particular favourite, invoked for the theft of a hair comb.

Even so, she felt that the tablet for the brooch was an advance on anything she had managed before. It read:

'Totia to the goddess Sul. I give to your divinity and majesty my magnificent serpent brooch, foully taken by someone with the probity and virtue of a destitute Parthian born into the lowest of all the houses of ill repute specialising in anal activities and worse. So long as this someone, whether slave or free, keeps silent or knows anything about it, may she – no names, Cambria – be accursed in her blood and eyes and every limb and even have all her intestines quite eaten away slowly by three large slugs if she has stolen the brooch or been privy to the theft. And further may dreadful death swiftly follow for whomsoever wears the brooch without your accedence.'

Now let me explain some pertinences about the curse tablets. First, you will notice that they address Sul, not Sulis Minerva. This is because the nominal merging of Sulis with the Roman goddess was the merest of lip services to the Latin invaders, who in truth worshipped nothing but themselves and certainly not their mad emperors or the more traditional divinities whose laughably wide portfolios demonstrated this lack of conviction. Minerva: goddess of wisdom *and* warfare;really? And this before her other supposed patronages: poetry, medicine, commerce, weaving. Her symbol both the owl and the serpent? Come on.

Sul is not like that. The druids, sensibly, chose to

follow but the one god. A god of the sun and moon, of fire and ice, of good and evil. One god combining opposed qualities, like humanity itself. One god with two persons, one for the light side, one for the dark. Christianity tried to follow this, but had to invent a third, frankly unsatisfactory person to distinguish itself and disguise its disingenuities.

So: Sul is the dark one, the moon, Sol the light, the sun. Solsbury Hill, Salisbury, Solent, Solway. Not so many places honouring Sul, but that's not perhaps surprising. Big at Bath, though: Aquae Sulis. But a misunderstanding, a touch of etymological, grammatical and theological confusion further muddied by the fiddling Romans with their multicultural meddling. Sol and Sul: not that difficult a concept, surely. Yet people still puzzle about the stone head in relief with wings and snakes that surmounted the temple, the one they call the Gorgon's Head, even though it seems to be a man when Medusa was a woman. Two things: gender fluidity is not a modern development; and that is the face of Sol. You do not want to see the face of Sul. Nobody wanted, wants, to see that. I know.

Totia was soon dead. Fittingly, she was a bitten by a viper, but nobody paid any attention because she was between slaves and they thought it was that dreadful laugh, not a cry for help. Did I mention that the curser dies as well as the cursed? Only fair. Most people worked that out in the end, although a few still try it today, with inevitable result, I'm not afraid. Cambria, too. She hadn't stolen the brooch back, but the curse is retrospective. She shouldn't have had it in the first place, end of. There are no nice distinctions in retribution. She was seized by a terrible thirst and drank herself to death on the hot spring water.

I expect that you have worked out who I am by now, too, and how I know such a lot about all this. I am Sul. Death follows me. And I tell the truth: there is no overworld or underworld after me, no place to carouse or consume foie de gras to the sound of trumpets, nor even to enjoy the company of whatever supreme being in which you have misplaced your beguilingly innocent but essentially stupid trust. After the sight of me, oblivion is all, and all the more welcome.

Not all see me, of course. I am more discerning than that. I don't attend to all curses. Even the Christians don't promise that their god answers all requests. But some things bring me. The Ouroboros for one. My symbol. Stolen by the Egyptians. The brooch is a particularly fine example. A bringer of death long before Totia's clumsy, vulgar attempt. It was given to Bladud by the druids, but the old fool didn't believe. If ever a flight was doomed, the doddery Trojan's leap off his idolatrous Temple of Apollo on Solsbury Hill was it. Lear didn't do too well, either, did he? After that, it found its way back to the druids. The arch-druid Myrrdin was wearing it when the Romans arrived on Mona. It was Myrrdin's mistake to think he had the power to summon me. Me. He should have kept to his oak and mistletoe. The legionaries watched him die, aghast at the look on his face. But they hadn't seen me, reflected in their shields. The Ouroboros then found its way to Boudicca, who tried to bargain with me. Me.

Such a lot of deaths. It's what I do. I won't bore you

with the brooch's complete history, as even terrifying extinction can become a touch repetitive. After Boudicca, three legionaries met me before it was stolen back by Cambria's father from my baths, where he was working as a masseur before he retired to a single storey dwelling in Gwynedd. He didn't long enjoy it. The brooch has had dormant periods, buried to keep it away from passing Angles, Saxons, Jutes and Monks, who were lucky.

But it does keep turning up. A few selected highlights: William Rufus, killed in the New Forest, 1100, accidentally shot with an arrow by a courtier; nonsense, it was punishment for allowing my city of Bath to be sacked by rebels and then presenting it to John of Tours, not only a quack, the Conqueror's doctor, but a cleric, the builder of the Christian temple far too near too mine. Greedy, too. He somehow 'acquired' the brooch after the Red One's death, and paid for it with a sudden 'heart attack' after supper when he saw me reflected in his silver. Then, owners of the brooch came from the rich and ruling. The Black Prince, Henry V, Richard III, Charles I, they all liked their jewellery. Nelson was the last hero to meet me. He was given the brooch in Bath by an ignorant admirer who thought it might remind him of the Nile. He had it from the estate of John Wood, who acquired it from the great grandson of one of the leading regicides. What a pity the great architect had to die before he could see the Circus and the Crescent complete. But it is possible to know too much.

And now? You are of an age which places little value on antiquity: anyone can afford the brooch; anyone can die, like the woman in London Road. I must say I like the serendipity, the randomness of this; that's why, occasionally, too, I like to kill someone for absolutely no reason. I never catch anyone completely unawares, though, that would never do: there has to be some terrifyingly insistent foreboding for a truly horrible death. In the lead-up to a tragic demise, my victim will become increasingly aware of Something. Something just beyond the corner of the eye. Something dark and threatening that can't quite be made out in the dusk. Something the soon-to-die thought they saw a couple of times there in the room, in the corner, as they awoke. That's me.

Classicists among you will recall that Medusa, the Gorgon, caught up in my story by legacy of the ignorant Romans, turned those who saw her into stone, such was the horror of her gaze. Perseus slayed her by using his shield as a mirror. But Medusa was a mortal. I am not. And it's the opposite with me, a superior form of horror, I like to think, as you never know when I might turn up in a reflection, in a shop window, on your mobile phone, mirrors everywhere, rearview, hotel bedroom, hotel bathroom, lift, you just can't avoid them, can you? The last clue to me is my smell, rich, slightly sickly, loamy, dead lilies and old rose. Unmistakeable, but too late. The brooch, by the way, is still in the gutter on London Road, waiting.

Afterword

THOSE WHO VISITED AND FREQUENTED THE BATHS *and Temple at Aquae Sulis were accustomed to cast offerings to the great goddess into the sacred spring in the corner across the courtyard from her Temple. By the time of Totia, the spring had been enclosed and roofed using oak piles that survive to the present day. Visitors gave thanks to the goddess or asked her to grant favours, including the imposition of fell punishments on enemies and thieves, known and unknown. These requests, inscribed on pieces of pewter, are known as 'curse tablets'; the first was found by the Bath City Architect, Major Charles Davis (qv), during the excavations in the late nineteenth century which uncovered the Roman complex. This is a typical example: 'Docilianus [son] of Brucerus to the most holy goddess Sulis. I curse him who has stolen my hooded cloak, whether man or woman, whether slave or free, that... the goddess Sulis inflict death upon... and not allow him sleep or children now and in the future, until he has brought my hooded cloak to the temple of her divinity.' Finds, including curse tablets, earrings, silver, gold and* bronze cups, some of the 20,000 coins, and an astonishing gilt bronze head of the goddess are on display to great effect at the Roman Baths Museum.

The Temple had steps leading up to four large columns topped by a decorated pediment which can be seen at the Museum and which was dominated by the carved stone Gorgon's Head. A large door led inside to the cellar where the cult statue of the goddess was kept in flamelit gloom. The Temple survived four centuries of Christianity until Theodosius ordered all pagan places of worship closed in 391 AD. After that, it fell into decay and collapse until its rediscovery and virtual restoration now on display.

The Great Bath in which Totia and her friends cavorted was fed with hot water directly from the Sacred Spring. Then, it had an enormous barrel-vaulted roof forty metres above the water. After some debate over the expense, the Victorian restorers of the Bath decided against rebuilding the roof and introduced the present scheme featuring statues of Rome's emperors and governors of Britain. It was one of a series of baths on the site which also featured the splendidly named Laconicum, the original sauna.

The leading characters in the story are all fictional. Hopefully.

See:

The Roman Baths, Abbey Church Yard, Bath BA1 1LZ (romanbaths.co.uk)

Read:

Roman Bath Discovered, Barry Cunliffe, 1971.

Alfred Speaks!

Record of the presence of Alfred the King at Hat Bathu, sometimes known as Bath, August, 891 (freely translated).

As everyone knows, Alfred, King of Wessex, King of all the Anglo-Saxons, is a legendarily busy man, with a great deal to be busy about. In the twenty-five years since he became king, he has defeated the Vikings at least five times over, reformed the army, central and local government, the law, the education and tax systems, founded the Royal Navy and Oxford University, written several books and translated more into English, fathered five children, and still found time to be acclaimed as the finest hunter of his generation. It was a remarkable honour, then, when the King was briefly in Aet Badum last week to be granted an audience during which His Majesty consented to answer a number of questions about his approach to ruling and winning.

Before the transcript of this unprecedented question and answer session, it might be useful for those who have not encountered the King (luckily, should you happen to have arrived in a longboat!) if we give a brief description of his appearance and characteristics. Alfred is tall, slender, in his forties, with a good head of hair which is now understandably streaked with silver. He could not be called conventionally good looking – his brow is too large for that – but his eyes, the palest of blue in colour, are remarkably bright and searching, except when he is pondering the answer to a question, when he seems almost in slumber. At all other times he is alert and never still, drumming his fingers, twitching a leg, looking around him, quick to smile, quick to frown. He sipped continually from a goblet. In between answering these questions, the King also gave dictation to five clerks on matters as diverse as wool prices and free will. His voice is melodious but still bears slightly sibilant traces of the continental accents of his forebears.

The Transcript

Q. *Good day, Sire, and welcome to Hat Bathu. Can you tell us the purpose of your visit today?*

A. Certainly. We're strengthening the defences here. They were thrown up in rather a hurry when our esteemed Norse cousins were having difficulty accepting that the English have a right to England. We, of course, have no difficulty accepting immigration, but we do think it needs to be controlled, which translates, essentially, into a feeling that requests accompanied by the point of a sword, the blade of an axe and excessively loud, guttural and threatening noises are simply not on.

Q. *Haven't the Vikings now accepted that, though? I thought that the Treaty of Wedmore and the Treaty of Alfred and Guthrum, which followed your stunning successes at Edington and Chippenham, recognised the peaceful co-existence of the Danelaw in the East and Wessex in the West? And now the Vikings have converted to Christianity, there is surely no longer any reason to fear them?*

A. Well, yes, up to a point. I would suggest that it is perhaps a little early to judge whether Christianity is an entirely peaceful religion. Old habits die hard, I find, and our Norse cousins do continue to enjoy a scrap, as anyone visiting Jorvik on a Saturday night will readily confirm. Moreover, the first duty of your government is to provide security. Which is why we're using a lot of the old Roman stones lying about to build some proper walls. It's the right thing to do.

Q. *Some have said this shows a lack of respect for the past?*

A. And I get that. But we can't recreate the past. That would be false. I greatly admire the Romans, and they built a splendid city here, but they didn't have much respect for old Bladud's stuff, did they? Ruthless people, with a hard edge of brutality. And I cannot be alone in finding Latin less than fit for purpose. Tough grammar, far too many rules. English is so much more flexible, and beautiful. Remember what the bard said about these very ruins here: 'Wondrously wrought and fair its wall of stone; fates broke it; courtyard pavements were smashed; the work of giants is decaying. Roofs are fallen, ruinous towers…' Do you see: we've taken Latin and run with it. That's what my translations are about. Very much a work in progress, of course. And don't worry, I'm working on the terrible spelling.

Q. *Good to be back in Bath?*

A. Very good. In a sense, this is where it all began for me. Round here. This part of Wessex was where I spent a lot of my childhood, and it was to here, after

I escaped with only my life from the massacre in Chippenham, that I returned, to the royal lands at Athelney. A hard time, but hard times are good for a king.

Q. *You know what I'm going to ask now. The cakes?*

A. Ah, yes, the cakes. They certainly follow me about, don't they? I'm not going to deny it happened on my watch, but there are mitigating circumstances. For a start, I was dog-tired and rather taken up with working out how to save my country. And though I was scolded roundly by my gracious peasant hostess, Berryngaria, for allowing them to burn, I hope I'm not thought too ungallant if I point out that she wasn't entirely blameless herself. Her slightly stodgy recipe left the cakes vulnerable to heating up on the outside too quickly and her pan was too small, causing uneven heat circulation. And instead of making the best out of a challenge, as I was doing with our Norse cousins, rather than just trimming off the edges and covering them with a honey, cream and butter frosting, she chose to turn a drama into a crisis. Nor can it be denied that she has subsequently done very well out of telling her story and opening Ye Sleepy King Tea Shoppe. Not that I begrudge her any of it: that sort of enterprise is what we need more of in this country if we're to improve our trade balance with the Danelaw, Europe and the rest of the world.

Q. *Is Hat Bathu doing enough in this regard?*

A. I'm glad you asked me that. Hat Bathu, or Bath, as I prefer to call it, is a remarkable place. I never fail to take a bath when I'm here as I'm a martyr to my bad back. And rheumatism, too much campaigning, sleeping in damp clothes, and the rest of it. Don't ask about the feet, either. I find a Bath bath really helps. Really helps. So this is a great place. And it has a great history. But forgive me if I sometimes wonder whether it doesn't dwell just a little too much on that great history. You have the potential to be a top destination, but you need to tidy up the rubble – our wall is going to help with that – and greatly increase visitor numbers. There also needs to be more strategic thinking about how the town can improve its offer – better baths, mixed baths, massage? I know there's a worry about attracting too many of our Norse cousins, but historically they've much preferred to be on water than in it. No, we should be after staycationers and Europeans. And, tell me, has anyone thought about drinking the water?

Q. *Why would anyone want to do that? It tastes terrible. Is that what you're drinking?*

A. Good grief, no. This is Somerset cider vinegar mixed with Somerset honey. Very good for indigestion. I'm a bit of a martyr to that, too, I'm afraid. The price of all these heavy state dinners.

Q. *Talking of the state, how are your reforms going?*

A. So, as you will know here in Bath, we've introduced a unitary system of boroughs which, although primarily concerned with the defence of the realm, will be much more efficient at realising the substantive and freely given expression of the common duty to support the kingdom.

Q. *What is the substantive and freely given expression of the common duty to support the kingdom?*

A. Tax.

Q. *You're raising taxes? No one told me!*

A. Read my lips. We've got, as you can readily understand, a pretty big defence budget. I've introduced a standing army to supplement the local volunteers. Nor can you fortify thirty-three boroughs, including Bath, without spending money. And that was before I founded the entire Royal Navy.

Q. *Wouldn't it be easier just to pay them to go away?*

A. And that is called paying the Dane-geld; but we've proved it again and again, that if once you have paid him the Dane-geld, you never get rid of the Dane. Appeasement is never the answer, ask any good leader at any time. We must always remember our history. That's why I'm so keen on learning. Ask me my three main priorities for government, and I tell you: education, education, education. For without wisdom there can be neither prosperity nor success in war. Every Englishman must learn who we are and who we should be.

Q. *Every Englishman?*

A. Yes. I have an ambitious programme to end slavery and serfdom by 900. Female emancipation may take a little longer.

Q. *Can't you just pass a law?*

A. Laws are the expression of the general will. Governments that fail to grasp that will find themselves in trouble. A leader can lead but he must know his people will follow.

Q. *So you ask them what they want?*

A. By the mass, no! Any leader who does that is abdicating his responsibility as well as being a fool of the highest order. People don't want to be bothered with the details, that's my job. Besides, they are quite likely to give the wrong answer.

Q. *I can tell you founded Oxford. Any advice on winning?*

A. Hmmm. When I started in this game, I used to be one for the full-on attack, the reckless surprise, the charge like a wild boar that won me the day at Ashdown. But if my career has taught me anything, it's that isolated, short-term gains are meaningless, that the best approach is to stay calm, resolute and obdurate; to be prepared for the swift and unexpected; and never to lose sight of the overall objective: in short, if you will allow me my little joke, always keep your eye on the cakes.

Q. *Very good, Sire. But while we're back on the cakes, there's a persistent rumour that Athelney wasn't the first time. A stew in Wantage?*

A. Fake news, my friend, fake news.

Q. *How do you wish to be remembered?*

A. It's a bit early to be talking about that! Not as some Saxon barbarian, obviously; otherwise, great. And I'll just say that it has always been my wish to live honourably, and after my death to leave to those who come after me my memory in good works. And do have a look at the *Anglo Saxon Chronicle,* it's all in there, cracking read.

Q. *Some people say the* Chronicle *is not entirely objective, that it exaggerates your achievements?*

A. I try to rise above the petty jealousies of lesser people. Or I kill them. That's another joke, by the way, possibly.

Q. *Mercians or Norsemen?*

A. Ungenerous hearts and small minds are exclusive to no race. Besides, I married a Mercian, a situation that does have its comedy moments. My wife, Ealhswith, affects to find West Saxons uncouth, while I point out that many of her people appear to be still pagan. I do steer clear of Mercian jokes, though, you know, what do you call a Mercian with a book, how many does it take to change a cartwheel, that sort of thing.

Q. *Do you ever compare yourself with another great king – Arthur?*

A. Who?

Q. *Arthur of the Britons?*

A. Oh, you mean the minor cavalry leader who was so successful at keeping us Saxons out? My only concern here is that the two names are very similar, which could lead to all manner of confusion in the future. You know how if they can make a mistake, monks will. They'd do better to concentrate on their prayer and scribing and stop bleating about our Norse cousins. Probably end up giving Arthur my round table and send pagans on some bizarre quest for the Holy Grail. Monks! And now I really must get on.

Q *Well, thank you so much for your time, Your Majesty, it's been a privilege.*

A. All mine, all mine. And make sure your report is as accurate as those in the *Chronicle*.

Afterword

A LFRED, YOUNGEST OF THE FIVE SONS OF KING
*Aethelwulf of Wessex, was born at Wanatage, now Wantage,
in 849. He became King in 871 after the death of his brother,
Aethelred, in the midst of the Viking invasions. After
early successes, including his headlong routing charge at
Ashdown, Alfred nearly lost his life in an unsporting Viking
raid on his palace in Chippenham at Christmas, 877–78. He
fled to Athelney to rally his forces and eventually defeated
the Viking leader, Guthrum, at the Battle of Edington in the
same year. Guthrum and his chief men agreed to convert
to Christianity, and the Treaties of Wedmore, and of Alfred
and Guthrum, effectively partitioned England between the
West Saxons and the Vikings, who retreated to the Danelaw
in the eastern half of the country.*

*During the relative lull in the fighting which followed,
Alfred re-organised his army, enlarged his navy, secured
London and instituted important reforms in the law,
administration and education. He established a court school
for his children and others, arguing that 'without wisdom*

there can be neither prosperity nor success'. Although famously illiterate until he was twelve, he translated several books from Latin into the burgeoning local vernacular, making him, if you'll forgive me, the sine qua non *of English, England and Englishness. He fought off further Viking incursions between 892 and 898. He died in 899. His grave has never been found.*

Various well-loved legends of Alfred have been called into doubt by more scrupulous research. The story of the cakes appears to be a twelfth-century invention. He did not found the Royal Navy: that honour seems to belong to his oldest brother, King Aethelstan of Kent, in a successful engagement with the Vikings off Sandwich in 851. For want of complete certainty, University College, Oxford's first, has graciously and rigorously waived a finding in fact in a court case of 1727 that Alfred founded it. Others of us, less in thrall to the idea that an absence of evidence is conclusive of its non-existence, wonder how these stories arose in the first place.

Although, as well, there is no evidence that Alfred was a hypochondriac, he did suffer from ill-health all his life; the suggestion by some medically inclined with no music in their souls that he had piles seem ungallant and quite unnecessary. At one time, he was also credited with many more translations. My own scruples force me to temper his claims to saintly universal social reform by pointing out that I made up his views on slaves and serfs and that his championing of education fell a little short of modern aspirations: 'to set to learning (as long as they are not useful for some other employment) all the free-born young men now in England who have the means to apply themselves to it'. Positively Etonian, then.

Until Alfred, all that remained of Aquae Sulis after the decline of Romano-Britain was a small monastic settlement with baths attached, its uncertain status emphasised by its many (water-derived) names: Aquaemann, Akemannceaster, and, eventually, Hat Bathu. The poem quoted by Alfred, 'The Choir', an old English poem, is wistfully elegiac about how far the once mighty resort had fallen from its days of glory, and is a reminder that nostalgia has always been what it used to be. Compare it with Shakespeare's 'bare ruin'd choirs' after the dissolution and destruction of the monasteries by Henry VIII and Thomas Cromwell.

It was Alfred who saved the city and began its restoration, in best vigorous Alfredian fashion. He made it one of his thirty-three fortified boroughs, or burghs, mutually reinforcing garrisons to check any further Viking ambitions. An emergency wooden wall had been hurriedly thrown up around the city, followed by more permanent repairs and consolidation of the old stone wall and its four compass-point gates, recycling the old Roman materials. He laid out a main or high street between the north and south gates, which ran round the old wooden Saxon abbey on the site of its stone successor; smaller roads radiated out to a circular relief road that survives in small part as Upper and Lower Borough Walls. The gates are now all gone, condemned by their narrowness, with the exception of the East Gate, which can still be seen at the medieval street level, down by the famed weir on the Avon below Pulteney Bridge, successor to the weir first introduced as a flood control measure in late medieval Bath. Remnants of the wall can be seen in Upper Borough Walls and in Old Orchard Street, in the delivery area of Marks & Spencer. (Modernity can be so heartless: you will recall Richard III under a carpark in Leicester; Henry I is supposed to be under another one in Reading.)

The Anglo-Saxon Chronicle *mentioned by Alfred was initiated by the king and is the single most important source for events in Britain from the arrival of the Romans to that of the Normans. He was rightly proud of it, but its scholarship was never above what an old journalistic acquaintance of mine used to describe as 'shepherding the facts'. The* Bath Chronicle *has been published under various names since 1743 and is now a weekly.*

See:

> *The Eastgate, 6 Newmarket Row, Bath BA2 4AN.*
> *Old Orchard Street, BA1 1JU, section of the old Roman Wall, modified by Alfred and in medieval times. Car park next to Marks & Spencer delivery area.*

Read:

> Life of King Alfred, *by Bishop Asser, 893.*
> The Anglo-Saxon Chronicle, *c880.*
> The Saxon and Norman Kings, *by Christopher Brooke, 1984.*
> In Search of the Dark Ages, *by Michael Wood, 2005.*

The Cook's Tale

IT WAS INDEED A DAY WHEN FOLK LONG TO GO ON
pilgrimages. A morning when spring has so sprung that
the bird song seems clearer, the jingle of harness sharper,
voices carry further, and the awakened sun shines on the
dew of the new. A morning full of hope and promise. A
morning to make even the humblest fellow fancy himself
in love.

This had been just another pilgrimage to Roger
until he saw Alison at The Tabard Inn in Southwark.
What a fine, wonderful woman! A pilgrim travelled
far and wide, from Santiago to Jerusalem. Not young,
but who wants the fresh and the green when the richly
matured and seasoned can be had? Roger, as you might
tell from his choice of image, was a cook. But Alison, he
thought, was a goddess, Juno at least. Her gown of rich
ruby fitted her full, voluptuous body where it touched,
and it touched everywhere. Her magnificent bosom
seemed in a constant and exciting struggle with its velvet
constraints. An elaborate wimple, topped by a broad hat,

almost concealed her hair, coloured blonde by celandine. Her face was of a strawberry and cream complexion with amused blue eyes. When she laughed, which was often, she revealed beguiling dimples and a sweet gap between her front teeth. Roger was a man smitten.

Things, though, did not go well, right from the start. Roger had hoped to make easy acquaintance of Alison as they rode along, a practised sally here, a droll aside there, as they began their ride to Canterbury and the shrine of the martyr Becket. The trouble with this approach was that Roger had neither the tongue nor the horsemanship to carry off the ploy, particularly as the ostler at The Tabard, handsomely tipped elsewhere, had given him a horse with a pronounced lean to the left. When he enquired, sarcastically, whether the steed was named Pegasus, the ostler replied, 'No, he's called Lurche,' which made everyone laugh, including, gallingly, Alison.

Furthermore, the pilgrimage's leader turned out to be none other than the genial mine hoste of The Tabard himself, Harry Bailey, who had been less than genial when a difference had arisen quite recently over the exact antecedents of the jelly in a batch of meat pies Roger had supplied to the inn. Worse, with his usual bonhomie restored, Harry had suggested that everyone should tell a story as they rode along, with the best tale-teller to be treated to a slap-up meal at The Tabard on their return. This sort of thing was definitely not Roger's metier; his rugged charm was not really up to romantic reverie; his skill was with the skillet. He rather suspected that the lettered and foppish toff accompanying them, one

G Chaucer, had suggested it to Harry, who was usually more interested in jests of the off-colour kind.

So he struggled along in the rear on Lurche while the pilgrims listened to the first tale, told, naturally, by the Knight, who was insistent on his status (as if surviving fifteen Crusades was much to brag about, thought Roger: Sir Fussfancy should try Billingsgate on a Friday). Most of the party – the merchant, the clerk, the lawyer, the other functionaries and the usual endless numbers of clergy – seemed to enjoy his tedious, extremely lengthy and, frankly, in Roger's opinion at least, unconvincing tale of hidden identity, courtly love and divine intervention. Alison in particular was most appreciative and attentive, to Roger's further chagrin.

The less elevated pilgrims, who tended to the rear, were not quite so impressed, and sought diversion from what one of them, the Miller, described as 'alle dis chivalrie bollokes'. (Worry not, further cod Olde English will be kept to a minimum.) And so, despite the early hour, a trenchering amount of sack was taken on board by him and his friend the Reeve and, of course, Roger. This necessarily contributed to a lowering of the tone in the tales told by the Miller and the Reeve after the Knight had finally finished somewhere near Greenwich with the exquisite sufferings of a couple of over-excited Greeks. Instead of the Knight's love, valour and suffering, the Miller and the Reeve provided pranks, bare bottoms, farts and vigorous couplings.

Roger enjoyed this and the sack so much that he thought he would give it a go himself, as it was certain to impress Alison. Sadly, it is one of the ironies of sack that it encourages confidence while diminishing performance, in every sense. And Roger would have been fully stretched in the story-telling department even if he had not been leaning to the right to balance Lurchee's inclination while at the same time juggling with the reins and the sack bottle. It was never going to go well. Magnificently undeterred, even by some barracking from Harry Bailey which cast aspersions on his catering and food hygiene standards, Roger embarked on a tale of a feckless London apprentice.

Perhaps you are unlucky enough to know that feeling when, having drink taken, you realise that you are not being as funny as you thought you were. Perhaps you are also unlucky enough to know that feeling when, speaking in public, you begin to realise your audience is not reacting well to your thoughts, in this case on pimps and brothels. Perhaps you are also unlucky enough to know that feeling when, speaking in public, you realise that you have completely forgotten what you were going to say next: thus poor Roger.

And as if all that were not enough, he was now bursting for a piss. Overloaded with a burden that would have taxed even the mighty mind of St Thomas Aquinas, Roger succumbed to the inevitable and slowly slid off Lurche. The company howled with laughter apart from G Chaucer, who was busy taking ostentatious notes, and Alison, whose look of withering disdain completed Roger's misery, along with a nasty gash on his shin.

*

THEY WERE NOW WELL ON THEIR WAY TO DARTFORD. Decorum had been restored by the Man of Law, who had embarked on an uplifting and uncontroversial account of the astoundingly virtuous daughter of a Roman emperor and the rewards of her constancy despite gross injustice and cruel fortune. Roger could hear little of it: his fall and some necessary attention to his cut shin had left him some way behind the group, and Lurche was not showing any marked enthusiasm for the chase, possibly because of the weight of Roger's provender panniers, packed with this spices, sauces, preserves and the odd fowl (predictably, careful distribution had failed to cure the horse's leftish inclination).

His mind, abruptly cleared by the tumble, was in any case on other things, principally the unlikelihood of Alison, now dividing her attention between the Knight's son and the Merchant, ever entertaining his suit. He also had supper to prepare that night for his immediate employers, four Guildsmen on their first pilgrimage, as evidenced by their splendid new crimson livery and their obvious intention to impress. They were a Carpenter, tall and thin with an appraising eye; a Dyer, taller yet and bald; a Weaver, not so tall but rounder; a Haberdasher, short and slim; and a Tapestry Maker, shorter, stooped and squinting. It was a pity their number had not included a tailor, as their liveries did not fit as well as they might, particularly in the case of the Haberdasher, who was rather swamped and whose handsome cap kept falling over his eyes, a pronounced handicap when one is not a skilled horseman.

The Man of Law, who was giving the impression, common to his calling, of an unquenchable urge to talk as long as there is a listener left, finally droned to a halt and was congratulated by the Miller and the Reeve with bleary winks for including not one but two mothers-in-law in his tale. By now the party was arriving in Dartford, which was just as well, as their travel weariness was evident in the bickering that had broken out between Harry Bailey, the Parson and the Shipman about who might tell the next story, and had now moved on to personal remarks about Harry's language and the Parson's orthodoxy or rather want of it. Roger made his way to the inn's kitchen and was soon busy doing his best with a couple of chickens. Taking no chances after a challenging day, he decided to rely on potage of oysters followed by a well-tested recipe involving breadcrumbs and spices which had been passed on to him by an old soldier from deep in England's south.

It certainly went down well with the Guildsmen, who were accompanying it with increasing amounts of a good Bordeaux wine, much to the disdain of the Knight and his party, whose disapproval of drinking red wine with chicken was increased by the changing social circumstances which put the Guildsmen at financial advantage, and the paucity of their own fare, some unappetising Umble pies (indeed: tripe, mostly). They were drinking what passed as the *vin du maison*, thin stuff that pretended to be from the Rhine but owed more to a modest operation just outside Reigate. Small wonder that G Chaucer chose to pass by the Guildsmen's table and opine that the chicken looked exceptionally good, a hint ignored by the Guildsmen, which might not necessarily have been a good idea. Roger, who had joined their party, was now beginning to feel better after his earlier disasters; it seemed remarkably unfair, then, that Alison should choose this moment to sweep by on her way to join the Knight, giving it as her opinion that breadcrumbs were rather 'vulgayre'. Fortunately, the Guildsmen, still concentrating hard on their tucker, didn't hear; but Roger did. Mortified, he retreated to the kitchen to mope before stiffening himself and returning with his prize fig pudding and some rather fine custard tarts. These the Guildsmen accompanied with the local braggot, or spiced ale, while they embarked upon a intense discussion about what stories they might tell the next day. The Haberdasher was very keen to relate the fascinating story of the emperor in a faraway land who was tricked into wearing a suit made from nothing. The Weaver said he wanted to tell that one, and knew more about suits than the Haberdasher. The Dyer wanted to tell the true story of Joseph's coat of many colours, announcing that he intended to go into great technical detail that would surely fascinate the pilgrims: 'Who, pray, woulde not want to know how your absorption differs from your adsorption?' The Tapestry Maker, a man made romantic by studying his subjects, said he knew a wonderful story about the star-crossed lover in Mantua who poisoned himself after thinking that his love was dead rather than just sleeping heavily. The Guildsmen all agreed this was too far-fetched, even for Italians. The Carpenter became most excited by something about a walrus, a whiting, a snail, oysters, cabbages and kings, but he was judged to have drunk too much braggot.

Meanwhile, back down in the kitchen, Roger was easing his ache of heart and desire by preparing some exquisite fare for the next day: a larded crane, gruel of almonds, blanched mortrews and some succulent bake-meats which exhausted the inn's entire stock of sparrows, bitterns and blackbirds. He worked into the night, for he knew sleep does not come easily to a passionate man whose shin was hurting.

*

THE NEXT MORNING WAS AS FINE AS THE FIRST, ANOTHER happy commingle of sun and sweet sounds and a breeze gentle enough to kiss the cheek and lightly stir the leaves into dapple. The Guildsmen did not seem to be enjoying it quite as much, though. The Carpenter was especially pale. The Merchant, an independent trader and fancily dressed fellow in varied colours, a beaver hat and a forked beard, was exhibiting all the characteristics of that well-known phenomenon, the man away from home with a hangover, mixing talk of money and successful deals with complaints that his wife didn't understand him. Still, once he had forgotten himself, he told a telling tale about the impossibility of old and young love because of the vanity of the old and the deceit of the young. G Chaucer again seemed to find this very interesting, and was again busy making notes on his wax tablet, which rested on a small lectern ingeniously attached to his saddle's pommel. Roger, whose long and sleepless night had been spent with many thoughts, now managed to nudge Lurche alongside the attentive scribe, and interrupted him: 'Sire, I have watched you, and I saw you laugh copiously yesterday when I unaccountably fell off my horse. I also see you writing things down. I know what you writers are like, having a fine time at the expense of honest folk. If you tell me my upset will go no further I will give you some of my excellent cold larded crane to fend off the pangs of the day.'

G Chaucer seemed a touch distracted, possibly because the Merchant was in the middle of a particularly interesting part of his story as the old man, January, who had been struck blind, allowed his young wife, May, to use his back to climb up a tree to meet her lover and indulge in some enthusiastic and frankly described congress. 'Just a minute, Goode Cooke,' he said, and continued scribbling, muttering to himself. 'Hmm, a bit strong. I wonder if I could get away with it.'

When he had finished, he looked up and gave Roger a winning smile. 'Goode Cooke, I would absolutely love some slices of larded crane. I did not dine as well as your party last night, tenches in gravy being not altogether to my taste. And you are clever to see that I am writing about this pilgrimage. My plan is to describe all the tales told on the way and back from Holy Canterbury. The story will end with the slappe-uppe supper in The Tabard which someone else is going to have to do very well to take away from this Merchant.

'I would be more than happy to say nothing of your false start yesterday since I want to bring happiness with my writing not pain. The larded crane would also be very nice. Now, pray forgive me, the Merchant is clearly winding up to his conclusion.'

A reassured Roger fell back as the party carried on to Rochester, the horses at walking pace interspersed with the quicker stride named for Canter-bury whenever the Merchant wished to take a break to gather his thoughts. His tale was much admired; it certainly seemed to strike a chord with Harry Bailey, who voiced severe complaints about his own wife. Roger, who, as we've seen, supplied The Tabard from time to time, knew that this, as is so often the case, was but one side of the story. Nevertheless, he said nothing, as he was proceeding more prudently today, having eschewed strong drink, not something of which the Miller and the Reeve could be accused, as they were now into a ragged chorus of 'Shewe Me the Waye to Go Home'. And if they had not been holy men, it might have been thought that the Friar and the Summoner were pretty busy in the artificial stimulant area, too.

Harry now called upon the Knight's son, a preening youth with fine curls who was acting as his father's Squire. He embarked upon a fantastical tale of talking birds, brass horses and magical swords which was enthusiastic but rambling and, finally, faltering; thankfully it was brought to a merciful and polite end by the Franklin, a man not of high birth but some sensitivity, especially in regard to the embarrassment of youth and the English tongue. This didn't prevent Harry, like most landlords a sucker for a title, and clearly still upset by the Merchant's tale, grumbling at the kind old Franklin and demanding his story. This turned out to be a gracious affair of gracious people behaving graciously in the face of temptation to do otherwise.

Moral uplift imparted, the sun was high and the stage set for contrast, which was enthusiastically provided by Alison. Her prefacing remarks showed that she was well-named the Wife of Bath, it turning out she had been married no fewer than three times. It was not a demure performance; Alison defended her right to marry as often as she liked, and was looking forward to her fourth. It was lucky that Roger was still at the back of the party, as at this his round face took on the colour of a sunset in September. Nor did this doughty woman hesitate to describe what she looked for in a husband, which, to be as clear, was frolicking in return for financing, and she was quite willing to engage in the one to gain the other. The secret to a successful marriage, at least to her, she said, was for a husband to do what he was told and for a wife to accuse her husband of bad behaviour before he found out about hers, which was frequent. Her biggest challenge had been her third husband, whom she'd set her eye on at her second's funeral: he had boxed her ear so hard she was still deaf in it; but she had gained the upper hand by hitting him even harder.

What is the opposite of music to the ears? Poor Roger; each revelation was worse than the last as his goddess plummeted to earth. He prided himself on being a fair-minded and civilised sort of a chap; but this? Yes, he recognised that the object of his amour was feisty, free-spirited and clearly no wallflower, shrinking violet or simpering posy poser. But a harridan and a harpie with the heart of a whore and the right hook of a butcher? Poor Roger. Even Lurche sensed his despair and made an unsuccessful effort to follow a straight line.

Alison, oblivious to the wilted, crushed and seared Cook, then told her tale, an intriguing account set in the days of King Arthur weaving courtesy, coarseness and love into what seemed a traditional story of knights and damsels up to the point where the usual old hag was transformed into a beautiful woman, not by her husband's love but by his submitting to her will. Thereafter, she obeyed him in everything, an unconvincing ending rather subverted by Alison's earnest closing prayer that Jesus Christ should send wives young, vigorous and obedient husbands with the politeness to die before them.

As you might imagine, something of a silence followed the Wife's performance, as the pilgrims applied her philosophies to their own situations. It would be hard to say who was more scandalised, all the men or all the clerisy, male and female. The Second Nun had turned a fetching pink. G Chaucer's face had the raised eyebrows and happy smile of a man who has just struck gold. The Miller and the Reeve began a low mumble whose content was clear. The Friar and the Summoner, for their part, were more taken up with bickering in a fashion familiar to those familiar with ecclesiasticals, but were eager to tell their tales. The Friar began by praising

Alison, thus proving that he hadn't been listening, and then concentrated on disobliging the Summoner with a story of one of his corrupt fellows in the church courts being taken off by the Devil. The Summoner, gander up, responded with a lively account of a corrupt Friar being given a splendidly coarse gift by a dying man he is attempting to gull. G Chaucer much liked this one, too, especially the punch line, which I shall not spoil.

It was in fine good humour, then, that the pilgrims achieved Rochester and the famous inn, Ye Worlde is Thine Oystur, with its bustling stables, courtyard and galleried rooms above. The Guildsmen, now feeling slightly better and all secretly relieved not to have been called on by Harry Bailey, were served by Roger with Glazed Sops to start, followed by his blancmange of fish, bream in almond milk, and *Sauges Seynes*, pigs' feet in sage sauce. A marked reduction in alcohol intake was countered at the Knight's table, where they were drinking to forget the Gruel of Almonds and the Battered Heron. Once again Alison had joined them, but not without the occasional wistful look at Roger's offerings.

The Merchant, the Reeve, the Shipman, the Friar and the Summoner were soon asleep, slumped at their tables. Two days of pilgrimage were hard work. The Prioress and the Second Nun retired early and modestly. The Canon, the Monk, the Nun's Priest and the Parson were, naturally, discussing Kent's chances against Somerset in their upcoming contest. The Merchant was being important with a local contact. The Plowman was showing off his strength to the very pretty serving wench by carrying up a barrel of ale from the cellar on one shoulder. The Man of Law was disputing his bill. A few others might have been praying.

Roger had been hard at work, and was in no mood to join any of the rousing or drowsing parties. It was a fine night, starred, with a welcome coolness after the kitchen. He sat in a far corner of the courtyard, unnoticed by other pilgrims as they made their way to their chambers after supper, some alone, some stumbling a little, some together, giving way to loud cries and banging doors. Then Alison came into view, escorted by the Knight. Roger stared at them climbing the stairs; the suddenness of her appearance quite defeated the defences he had been hopelessly building. They paused at her door, Alison smiling at one of the Knight's sallies. Then he took hold of her and pulled her to him. Excellent, thought Roger grimly, first I am not so much dismissed as not even considered; now I am supposed to watch as Sir Rusty Swordsman wins the prize. His absorbing self-pity prevented him for a few moments from realising that the Knight's attentions were not being welcomed. Alison was struggling against the Knight, and not in any coquettish way. Cometh the hour, cometh Ye Cooke; Roger charged across the courtyard and bounded up the stairs at a pace which would have astonished him if he'd had time to notice it. Without a pause, he ran down the gallery and challenged the Knight, 'Unhand the lady, you old goat, you lecher, you very January!'

The Knight took little notice, continuing the struggle with Alison, pushing her against her door and bracing himself with one hand against it while putting the other over her mouth. 'Go away, sad little cook,' he growled over his shoulder, 'before I use the sword that has killed more Moors than you've burnt tarts to turn you into cuts of your meat. Now, then, my feisty one, let your next husband at you!'

Roger was not a brave man, but we all have our moment, that moment when outrage at a predicament conquers timidity and springs action. Roger, as we have seen, had been having a rough old time of it, and all his frustration, despair and rage went into the kick that now landed on the haughty titled one's backside. With a roar, the Knight swung round to face Roger, drawing his sword as he did.

'I've changed my mind, Cook,' he snarled. 'I'm not going to turn you into a neatly sliced assembly of ingredients, I'm going to turn you into that prized Saracen comestible, the kebab!'

We are also all familiar with that other moment, that moment when we realise we might have started something we might not necessarily be able to finish. Roger did not retreat, but he did feel a waver coming on. He had been hoping that Alison, no stranger by her own account to direct action and now freed from the Knight's grasp, might pitch in to help. But instead she was just standing there, frozen, silent, her mouth moving like a fish, a very attractive fish, admittedly, but still a fish, and about as much use in hand-to-hand combat.

Roger rallied. 'Do your worst,' he cried, 'you shrivelled old jouster!' The Knight obliged; Roger felt the tip of the sword at his throat, forcing him back towards the gallery's rail, with its long drop to the courtyard on the other side. Defeat, ignominy, his lady's honour and any number of broken bones stared at him from the Knight's purple face.

It was just then that he heard a calm voice say, 'I'd put that sword down if I were you, olde fruite.'

Roger and the Knight turned to face the voice and saw the Guildsmen lined close in single file and in order of ascending height: the Tapestry Maker, who had spoken, at the front; the Haberdasher behind the Tapestry Maker; the Weaver behind the Haberdasher; the Carpenter behind the Weaver and the Dyer behind the Carpenter. Five faces in the gallery's candlelight stared levelly one above the other at the Knight. He laughed that contemptuous laugh which never bodes well for the villain. 'What's this got to do with you, girls? Have you any idea how ridiculous you look in your silly red robes, you jumped-up money-grubbing sons of smelly serfs? Have away to your needles and pins before I stick you!'

The Knight then took a swift step towards them and struck with a flash of his blade, taking off a large slice of the Haberdasher's cap. The next few moments were mayhem as the Guildsmen hurled themselves at the Knight rather in the manner of a troupe of tumblers. The arrival of the Knight's son and his Yeoman added to the chaos, which would have been even worse if the ruder elements downstairs hadn't still been snoring and the clerical persuasion still engrossed in sporting affairs. Victory began to swing towards the Guildsmen when they were joined by the Plowman, whose first act was to toss the Yeoman over the rail into the courtyard below. He landed on the Friar, who happened to be passing; the Friar, naturally, let forth the most tremendous fart on the sudden impact which quite overcame the Prioress and the Second Nun, who had come out to see what all the noise was about and were too close behind.

Upstairs, the Tapestry maker then threatened the Son's curls with his scissors and a leering smile, more than enough to send the youth running as fast as his too-tight hose would allow. There remained the Knight, now pinned by the other four Guildsmen but still making the most terrific amount of noise and swearing the most dreadful punishments. Roger, seeing his chance, tickled him under the arm until he released his sword. This was picked up by the Plowman, who proceeded to beat the Knight hard on his already bruised backside before dispatching him towards his horse with a kick that excited even Roger's admiration. 'That,' said the Plowman with some satisfaction, 'was for 1381'.

As the Knight and his crumpled and crestfallen retinue left the courtyard, Alison came up to Roger. 'Goode Cooke,' she said, 'I owe you my honour and my life. How can I ever repay you?'

'Well,' said Roger, 'you could tell me why I had to take on that evil Knight single-handed apart from a nominal amount of help from the Plowman and the Guildsmen. What happened to your right hook?'

'Goode Cooke, there are things you must know. I have been married but the once, to my dearest Reginald, an undertaker who sadly drowned in the King's Bath in that city after slipping on a bar of soap. I have never been to Boulogne, Cologne or Santiago. Not only have I not been to Jerusalem three times, I have never been to Jerusalem at all. Until this pilgrimage, I had never been as far as Frome.

'But after Reginald's slippery end, it was increasingly borne in on me that I had not done enough with my life. So I resolved to sell my dear husband's business and travel round the world on pilgrimages, the first to Canterbury. It seemed wise to protect myself by pretending to more experience than I had, which was none. So I bought myself some new outfits, dyed my hair, hired a travelling servant, and made my way to Southwark. That was a journey! Thieves and villains, shysters and tricksters! But I learnt quickly, and was not even discountenanced when my servant, one Dick, announced he was turning again and staying in London to try his fortune.

'I came to The Tabard and felt safe in this party; safe enough, as you must have seen and heard, to enjoy my boasting and flirting and flouncing, my pretence to husbands and lovers and travel and all that bawdy business about the superiority of women and the need to keep men down, which is not what I believe. I believe that man and woman are equal and shall never be happy and content until they are treated and treat themselves so. No ruler and ruled, orderer and ordered, but give and take and friendship and gentle talk and honest consent and sweet agreement.

'So I was living a lie, and I suppose I rightly deserved that Knight, a pomped oaf who smelt. I suppose I deserve what was happening to me when you arrived, my guardian Cook. As you saw, I was so shocked, poor silly unworldly me, that I became rooted to the spot and could neither run, nor shout; and certainly not use my right hook, which is more of a flap. Can you forgive me?'

Well. Did I mention music to the ears earlier? Roger was still a man who could not believe his luck, but this was of the better kind. And he was still smitten. And that smittenness now lent him eloquence. 'Alison, hush. Rightly I knew from the moment I saw you that you were the only woman for me, the woman I had been waiting for all my life, the woman who made my previous fumbling and flirtations seem as worthless and meaningless as they were.

'Of course I knew the character you were affecting was not the true you.' [A man smitten is allowed a little licence, surely?] 'Will you come live with me and be my fair Wife of Bath, where we will be happy and agreeable and equal in everything?

Well. I think we might know what Alison was about to say when G Chaucer arrived, still pulling on his hose, detousling his hair and breathing heavily.

'What's been going on? Where is everybody?' He shouted.

'The Knight and his party have left, rather hurriedly,' said Roger. 'I'm afraid he was found behaving in a way unbefitting to his character and his tale.'

'Gone! They can't do that! It will ruin my plot! How are they going to tell more stories? This is a disaster! Where are the Guildsmen?'

'They have announced their intention to leave, having been grievously insulted by the Knight, and having learnt of my intention also to leave forthwith. They say that going on a pilgrimage is much tougher than they imagined – they particularly mentioned the company they have had to keep – and that it will be quite unbearable without my beguiling victuals. Please pass that on to Harry Bailey.'

'Why are you leaving?'

'I am leaving because, before you interrupted, my Lady Alison was about to agree to live with me and be my love in the fairest city of Bath. Certainly fairer than my home town, at any rate.'

'Where is that?' asked the distracted Chaucer, unable to contain his all-consuming curiosity even at this critical moment.

'Ware,' said Roger.

'I just asked *you* that!' shouted Chaucer, who was now beginning, as the vernacular has it, to really lose it.

'Ware, in Hertfordshire. Named after its weirs. An all right sort of a place, I suppose, but dull.'

'Roger,' said Alison. 'Yes. Let us leave now, my love.'

'Don't, please,' said Chaucer. 'Stay and I will make you immortal.'

'No,' said Alison. 'We are leaving, commanded by our ardency. Would you rather be immortal or loved?'

'But he's only a cook. And not exactly a looker.'

'Fie, such a thing from you, G Chaucer, glancer into hearts, seer of souls and diviner of the mysteries of gentle intent. As for immortality, I would fain not have my embellishments and exaggerations and inventions put down for all the world to know for ever.'

'There is a simple way to secure that, my fair lady. Stay and tell more stories and nothing of the first will survive.'

'The word has not yet been made for your dastardly proposal, but when it is, it will be an ugly one. One day I trust you will take all your badnesses back. Roger, come, we must make Southwark before Bath.'

And so they left into the night, side by side, Alison's mare finally keeping Lurche on a straight path. The light from the ostler's torch fell across G Chaucer's face as he watched them go, wryly rueful, with a freshly forming thought that he clearly found amusing.

Roger and Alison wed and prospered in Bath; it was remarked that between them there was no telling who was the leader and who was the led; or who was the more loved. Roger cooked and Alison span; they lived and worked close by the old Abbey and were a familiar sight at the market in High Street, where it would be equally hard to say which was the more popular, Roger's pies or Alison's robes. They did occasionally discuss going on another pilgrimage, but somehow never got round to it.

Afterword

GEOFFREY CHAUCER (1343–1400) CONCEIVED *that his most famous work,* The Canterbury Tales, *would feature some thirty pilgrims travelling to and from Southwark and telling two tales each way for a prize of supper at* The Tabard Inn *on their return. It is not clear why he abandoned this plan.*

In the work that survives, the tale of the Cook, named as Roger of Ware, breaks off after fifty-eight lines, similarly unexplained. He had indeed been hired by the Guildsmen, the arrivistes of the day.

There is no record of the romance between Roger and Alison. The other details of the pilgrims and pilgrimage are correct, except that Roger falls off his horse rather later on. Chaucer doesn't say where the party stayed along the route, but my guesses accord with the usual suggestions of Dartford, Rochester and Ospringe for overnight stops on the accustomed four-day journey.

Bath became an important centre for wool and weaving in the medieval period. Chaucer describes

Alison thus, 'Of cloth-making she hadde swiche an haunt, she passed hem of Ypres and of Gaunt' (she had such a skill she surpassed the weavers of Ypres and Ghent). Here Chaucer seems to be up to some typical teasing, as Bath actually had a poor reputation for quality.

Chaucer was also less forgiving about the problem with Roger's leg, making it a boil. And he gives Alison five husbands.

The Ploughman's mention of 1381 refers, of course, to the Peasant's Revolt, the rising up of the common English people against iniquitous taxation disdainfully imposed by the ruling classes to pay for their incompetent warmongering. The people were promised redress then shamefully betrayed by the young Richard II. Chaucer served the king and was in London when the Peasants marched into the city. He kept his opinion to himself, but it can be imagined.

One day, though, he did take all his badnesses back: the Tales end with his Retraction, 'Wherfore I biseke yow mekely, for the mercy of God, that ye preye for me that Crist have mercy on me and foryeve me my giltes; and namely of my translacions and enditynges of worldly vanitees...' (Wherefore I beseech you meekly, for the mercy of God, that you pray for me that Christ have mercy on me and forgive me my sins; and namely of my translations and compositions of worldly vanities...)

I'm sure Roger and Alison understood.

See:

> *High Street, BA1 5AQ, site of the original Bath market.*
>
> *Upper Borough Walls BA1 1RL, where a section of the medieval wall survives.*

Read:

> The Canterbury Tales, *by Geoffrey Chaucer, 1387.*
>
> English Wayfaring Life in the Middle Ages, *by JJ Jusserand, 1891.*
>
> The Time Traveller's Guide to Medieval England, *by Ian Mortimer, 2009.*
>
> Chaucer's People, Everyday Lives in Medieval England, *by Lisa Picard, 2016.*

Flushed

IN THE DAYS OF GOOD QUEEN BESS AND HER LESS blessed successor, there lived near Bath, in Kelston, a knight of grace and wit and learning easily the equal of any other man or woman in England. Sir John Harington was a writer and an inventor, a fine father, a loving husband, and a faithful friend. He was also very fond of his dog, which is always a good sign. He could turn an excellent epigram, pen a wise letter, and talk with wit and charm. He had generous impulses and good intentions. Both his writings and his most famed invention – of which more soon – deserved praise.

Yet Sir John did not become a great man. He never did attain a powerful position at court, despite his enduringly and endearingly optimistic endeavours, incessant approaches and splendid letters suggesting such. No Cecil, Howard or Walsingham, he. Neither did his sharp verse and glistering prose secure him a place alongside Shakespeare, Jonson, Spenser, Sidney, Campion, nor even Beaumont, Fletcher and those of that rank.

Why? How so? Because Sir John was, if you will, a knight benighted, a man beset by one great flaw; a flaw that has condemned many others through time and place: try as he might, strive as he would, Sir John was incapable of resisting a joke. Thus his intellect and seriousness were largely ignored by a world that ever for ease seeks simple single characteristics and motives. To his peers, Sir John was irredeemably, irrecoverably, *frivolous*.

And so the poet who laboured long to produce a staggeringly clever 33,000 line translation of one of renaissance Europe's chief literary glories, Ariosto's epic poem of chivalry and romance and magic, *Orlando Furioso,* is remembered, if at all, as the man who invented the water closet, with all the smirking and sniggering that attends.

Would he be upset by this? A little, perhaps, before he anticipated another poet of less robust turn, and talked about a name writ in water. We could ask him, but at present he is slumbering in the shade of a fine old elm on a Jacobean afternoon in late August, as befits a knight who has led a crowded life. Behind him, shimmering slightly in the heat, is his pleasing manor house, newly built by him, in the best Italian style, happily at rest above the Avon. It would be wrong to wake him, although he has always enjoyed company – perhaps too well!

What tales he could tell: of his beloved wife, Mary, called by him 'Mall'; of his seven surviving children; and his dog, Bungey, that clever Spaniel whose portrait, in a typically facetious touch, adorns the frontispiece of *Furioso,* but is now gone before, as dogs do; of life at court, under his adored godmother, Elizabeth, and the odd

James, whose favour was easier to gain if you were young and male, easier to lose if you omitted to compliment his learning or his horse. Elizabeth called Sir John, 'that merry poet, my godson'; for James, he was 'the merry blade'. But merriness is not always meritorious, then as now.

It would not be long, either, before he had moved on to his dealings with other favourites: haughty Leicester, who didn't like being teased for being jealous of another suitor, the Duke of Alencon; and the stupid doomed boy Essex, whose fateful expedition to Ireland almost lost Sir John his life, too. But he would never forget meeting the great rebel O'Neill – he read some *Furioso* to him, of course, and presented his young sons with a copy – or the desperate defeat of the English in Connaught's Curlew Mountains.

His godmother loved him, though, and forgave him everything, eventually. His mother and father had stood by Elizabeth at great risk to themselves during the reign of Mad Mary; Elizabeth did not forget. And she almost had his mark, suspected the seriousness beneath it all. When she found Sir John was introducing her ladies-in-waiting to his saucy translation of the lustier side of *Furioso* – lots of 'opening the paradise' and wielding of 'weapons' – his punishment was to translate the whole work.

And he did, after 'some yeeres, and months, and weeks, and dayes', before he was thirty. It was rightly well received, and he was rightly proud of it, promoting it wherever he could – see above – with grace and gusto. A good indication of its success and worth was that Ben Jonson so vigorously dismissed it. But, again, that implacable urge to jest would not be denied, and, in 1596,

Sir John published the work which exchanged literary acclaim for a more specialised fame: *The New Discourse of a Stale Subject, called the Metamorphosis of Ajax.*

Ajax was a play on Jakes, Elizabethan slang for the privy. *The New Discourse* is a remarkable work, combining satire, learning and literary diversion with detailed and frank instructions for the construction of a flushing closet employing a cistern above and a trap below, complete with detailed diagrams in woodcut. There is innuendo and double-entendre of the broad and belchy sort contained in the title; but what the work chiefly exhibits is the exuberant enjoyment at defying convention which so distinguished its age, and the seething, racing, overflowing mind of its author. Along with the copious references to figures of antiquity and the teasing of contemporaries no longer identifiable, there is a delight in vulgarity and nonsense that the more pretentious might choose to define as an essentially English humour (if they ignored that rude French fellow, Rabelais). And should you, even today, blanch a touch at Sir John's examination of different materials for arse-wiping, he reminds you of this enduring national inclination by pointing out the vital part in state affairs given to the Privy Chamber.

As if to prove his wit can't be contained, Harington also scribbled in his own margins. One joke displays the kind of humour that still displays today, when he advises that a sure way to keep a chimney from smoking and a privy from smelling is to make your fire in your privy and put your privy in your chimney. You will observe that here he is also arguing against the invention he purports to promote, but that is Sir John and his jokes again (in much the same way, he makes clear that the idea for his invention did not come to him sat in contemplation while engaged in the apt activity).

The New Discourse was published under a nom-de-plume – Misacmos, or a hater of fithiness – but Sir John, like all comics, couldn't resist making it clear that he was the cheeky chappie. It caused, as you might expect and can't expect me to resist, an almighty stink at court. The threat of the notoriously abrupt justice of the Star Chamber was narrowly avoided. But another lengthy period in Kelston ensued, until this arrived from a friend: 'Your book is almost forgiven, and I may say forgotten; but not for its lack of wit or satyr... and tho' her Highnesse signified displeasure in outwarde sorte, yet did she like the marrow of your booke ... The Queen is minded to take you to her favour, but she sweareth that she believes you will make epigrams and write misacmos again on her and all the courte; she hath been heard to say, "that merry poet, her godson, must not come to Greenwich, till he hath grown sober, and leaveth the ladies sportes and frolicks."'

And so the moments of favour, exile and alarum of the Tudor-Jacobean courtier continued on their dangerous way, including imprisonment for a relative's debt (he spent the time translating Book VI of *The Aeneid*). The most perilous moment came with Essex's failure in Ireland, subsequent treason and execution. It was Essex who had knighted him in the field, along with too many others, another reason for sovereign wrath. But once more he escaped, rescued by the charm that so often endangered him: 'I had a sharp message from her brought by my Lord Buckhurst, namely thus, "Go tell that witty fellow, my godson, to get home: it is no season now to foole it here."'

No season now to foole it here! But this is a fool who came out with the finest description of treachery yet rhymed: 'Treason doth never prosper: what's the reason? Why, if it prosper, none dare call it treason'. (Other epigrams pioneer now familiar territory by being rude to and about his mother-in-law, Lady Rogers; more costly humour, as she didn't see the joke and failed to make him her executor, leading to all sorts of trouble.)

But Sir John was back to read to his Queen – from his own work, naturally – as her life drew to its close, 'whereat she smilede once, and was pleasede to saie; — "When thou doste feele creepinge tyme at thye gate, these fooleries will please thee lesse. I am paste my relishe for suche matters."'

And, at her death, he was bereft: 'In soothe, I have loste the beste and faireste love that ever shepherde knew, even my gracious Queene... and sith my goode mistresse is gone, I shall not hastily put forthe for a new master... I wyll keepe companie with none but my sheep and cattle, and go to Bathe and drinke sacke, and wash awaie remembraunces of paste times in the streams of Forgetfulness.'

You will know someone like this, know how such people are; we all do. They succumb to their charm, too. (And he was, after all, one of the first Etonians.) So you will understand that the tribute is no less sincere because our incorrigible courtier had already been pressing his suit on that new master and his son, the young Prince Henry, who, like another Prince Hal, was clearly entertained by an old charmer. And what prince would not smile at a man who, in 1605, with his record, asked, apparently in earnest, to be considered for the position of Archbishop of Dublin?

But wait: under his tree, in his deckchair, Sir John stirs, and, above the goatee, white now, a smile plays on his lips, as if he is remembering that remarkable Irish application. (It failed, by the way.) Mall approaches with one of her ladies, surveys her sleeping squire, raises her eyes to the heavens, and retreats. The waft of woodbine, musk rose and sweetbriar hangs in the drowsy air, joined by the soothing sounds of the chaffinch, the willow warbler, and Tom Combe, Sir John's faithful old servant, making his rhythmic way with the Harington Super Ajax lawnmower.

Sir John loved Bath, and was entertained by its fandangos: this is a finely scurrilous piece of Harington:

Of going to Bathe
A common phrase long used here hath been,
And by prescription now some credit hath:
That divers Ladies coming to the Bath,
Come chiefly but to see, and to be seen.
But if I should declare my conscience briefly,
I cannot think that is their errand chiefly.
From what I hear of how most with Bath have dealt,
They chiefly came to feel, and to be felt.

In truth, though, he is being a little economical when he says his principal occupation in Bath will be drinking sack to forget. I will be far from the first to point out that the irresistible wit and cheek of this man concealed a moral purpose, religious faith and admirable tolerance (which perhaps makes his ecclesiastical ambition more readily understandable; or not). He cared for Bath as well as teasing it, complaining especially that a place so providentially provided with so much water should so fiercely attack the senses with its sanitary inadequacies. Indeed, on that great occasion when Elizabeth stayed with Sir John and he presented her with a magnificent copy of *Orlando Furioso*, the royal senses were fiercely attacked when she visited the city; which most likely explains his interest in Ajax.

Chiefly, though, he loved the Abbey, whose life has had yet more vicissitudes than his. Built by Saxons, burnt, rebuilt by Normans, ruined, rebuilt by Tudors, dissolved by Tudors, in Sir John's day its times were particularly uncertain. The great rebuilding begun by Bishop Oliver King under Henry VII had stuttered and stalled in the religious upheavals; it had been offered to the city of Bath, and they had refused, muttering about pigs and pokes; it had then ended up in the hands of the most literal of asset strippers, losing its lead, glass, roof and bells, before finally being returned to the Corporation, an empty shell.

In 1574, though, following her noisome visit, Elizabeth, ever cleverly steering the direction of the infant Church of England, gave her approval to that time-honoured English enterprise, the urgent church appeal for funds. Thereafter, her godson was mightily involved in the effort, and the results show evidence of the talent for promotion so evident with his books. The application that produced *Furioso* is to be seen in the many persuasive letters he wrote begging for the Abbey; this, for example, is to the mighty Lord Burghley, Elizabeth's renowned chief man of affairs:

> *'Our work at the Bathe dothe go on hand…
> we sometime gallop with good presents, and then
> as soon stand still, for lack of good spurring: but it
> seemeth more like a church than it has aforetime,
> when a man could not pray without danger of
> having good St Stephen's death, by the stones
> tumbling about our ears.'*

And this in 1608, after the death of both the old Queen and Burghley, but with evidence his appeals had not gone unheeded, is to Thomas Sutton, mine owner, moneylender, founder of Charterhouse School and reputedly the richest man in England:

> *'Do somewhat for this church; you promised
> to have seen it e're this; whensoever you will go to
> Bathe, my lodgings shall be at your commandmente:
> the baths would strengthen your sinews, the alms
> would comfort your soule. The tower, the quire,
> and two isles, are already finished by Mr Billett,
> executor to the worthie Lord Treasurer Burghley:
> the walls are up ready for covering. The leade is
> promised by our bountiful bishop, Dr Montague;*

timber is promised by the earl of Shrewsburie, the earle of Hartford, the Lord Say, Mr Robert Hopton, and others. There lacks but monie for workmanship, which if you would give, you should have many good prayers in the church now in your life-time, when they may indeed doe you good…' Notre Dame has no more distinguished benefactors.

I hope, too, that I might not be accused of a lack of religious feeling or an excessive amount of the cynicism of our age if I point out that all marketing operations have ever demanded a strong founding myth for the product. And so we come to one of Bath's great legends, ranking alongside the deeds of Bladud: Oliver's Dream.

This was the vision of Oliver King, the new bishop of Bath and Wells, trusted servant of God and Henry VII, not necessarily in that order, after he had discovered the parlous state of the near-derelict Norman Abbey and the less than ascetic goings-on of its monks. The slumbering bishop saw the Holy Trinity and a host of angels ascending and descending a ladder from Heaven, at the foot of which was an olive tree supporting a crown. And a voice spoke to him, 'Let an olive establish the crown and let a king restore the church'. And so it came to pass, particularly the truly wonderful West Front of the Abbey, complete with its appealing angels toiling up and down their ladders (they always made Sir John smile) and the olive trees, crowns and mitres in stone and honour of the bishop and his King, whose statue takes billing second only to that of Christ.

I should add, and certainly without further remark, that

the first reference to Oliver's Dream comes in the writings of one Sir John Harington of Kelston, around a century later.

The same Sir John Harington who is said to have persuaded the later, aforementioned and recently appointed Bishop Montague to finish the roof with the aid of some wiliness that certainly has a familiar ring to it. Taking advantage of the lucky chance of a rain shower – for, as all know, it rarely rains in Bath – Sir John took the bishop to stand in a particularly roof-challenged part of the Abbey: 'As this situation was far from securing his Lordship from the weather, he often remonstrated to his merry companion that it rained; "Doth it so, my Lord? Then let me sue your bounty towards covering our poor church; for if it keep not us safe from the waters above, how shall it ever save others from the fire beneath?" Hereat the bishop was so well pleased, that he became a most liberal benefactor both of timber and lead...' Clever Sir John. He seems to have got the bishop's brother to stump up for the West Front's magnificent door, too.

Some have also suggested that the authorship of the verse graffito Sir John describes on a wall of the suffering Abbey – a charity appeal in itself – was not quite as anonymous as he made it appear:

O Church! I wail thy woeful plight
Whom King nor Card'nall, nor Clerke not Knight,
Have yet restor'd to ancient right.

There – there is that smile again from Sir John; but still he does not wake. And if he cannot join us, then we should join him. He is in 1592, in the midst of one of his favourite reveries, of that visit to Kelston by his godmother the Queen, when he presented her with a special edition of *Furioso* and they dined in the courtyard under Kelston's glory, its fountain, raised high on pillars, its plashing waters in happy backdrop to the witty table; when creepinge tyme was still some way beyond the gate.

Such happenings! No wonder the knight slumbers on, and would perhaps still be sleeping now but for the intervention of his most ingenious steam-powered Harington Giddy Thee Uppe alarm clock, involving a sandglass egg timer and a feather duster that tickles a tethered cockerel. A little late, perhaps an hour, but, as Sir John says, for the dedicated inventor there will always be teething problems.

He stares for a moment, remembering his Queen: 'When she smiled, it was a pure sunshine.' Then he stands, stretches, strokes a stray deerhound and leads the way past the nodding violets and oxlips, and the knot garden of thyme, hyssop and lavender, to the fountain courtyard. The play of water soothes, accompanies the talk. He speaks of *Furioso;* and smiles proudly. He speaks of *The Discourse;* and smiles ruefully, but still fondly. He speaks of the interesting similarities between his works and the plots and characters and devices in *Othello*, *As You Like It* and *Much Ado About Nothing;* and just smiles. 'Met the fellow once, in Bath, good listener, unusual for an actor. He hailed me, "How now, Sir John!" I gave him some advice. I told him to keep his head down and stick to comedy!'

There is a whistling sound. Sir John claps his hands: 'Kettle's boiled! Time for tea!' Mall appears, followed by a servant bearing the beverage. They sip, this long-accustomed pair, silently companionable. What did he once write? 'I came home to Kelstone, and founde my Mall, my childrene, and my cattle, all well fedde, well taughte, and well belovede.'

The sun has shifted and lowered. 'I have nowe passed my storms, and wishe for a quiet harbour to laye up my bark,' sighs Sir John. 'For I growe olde and infirme. I see few friendes, and hope I have no enemies.' Though he has just passed fifty, Tudor times move swiftly. Mall tells him not to be a fool, but fondly, with a quick look, instantly disappeared, that foresees sad shades.

'So many things left undone,' he says, with a sigh. Perhaps he will not now get round to setting down the details of his many other pioneering ideas, like the lawnmower and the alarm clock: the Harington wind-powered spin dryer, for example; or the Harington Pop-Up Toaster, enlisting candles, a spring and two very patient – and agile! – servants. And what of his plan for a giant balloon? He will fly as high as Bladud – but for longer and more gently! – once he has refined his scheme to gather gas from his cows' backsides to fill it (slight problem with them floating away at present). Mall says he'll soon solve that, as hot air is his speciality. Sir John chuckles: 'Very good, Mall'. As if in salute, a Bath breeze comes up. Tom Combe, mowing done, rattles by, bound for the Crown, not Old then; he raises a hand in salute and his Harington twenty-eight-inch Furioso Fixed Gear makes the first wobble of the many that will follow after the Crown, on the way home to Swineford.

It is time to go in. Shortly after, there is the familiar sound of pulled lever and running water. The fountain stops abruptly. A meadow pipit joins a blackbird and a particularly lively song thrush in singing against the dusk; Sir John's geese honk at the rowdy returning rooks. Then all stills, and summer's eve comes to Kelston.

Afterword

THE GUIDING PRINCIPLE IN CONSIDERING THE LIFE *of SIR JOHN HARINGTON (1560–1612) is delightfully expressed by Jason Scott-Warren in Sir John's entry in the* Dictionary of National Biography: *'much of the foregoing biographical narrative should be treated with caution, since Harington is often our only source for what we "know" about him'. It is agreed, though, that his father, also John (1517–82), was first married to Etheldreda Make, a daughter of King Henry VIII born out of wedlock to Joanna Dyngley, through whom he acquired Kelston and the nearby manors of Batheaston and St Catherine's Court. And that his second wife, Isabella Markham, mother of Sir John, was a confidante of Elizabeth.*

There seems agreement that his water closet was installed at Kelston, and, less certainly, for the Queen and Sir Robert Cecil as well. Recent examinations of early editions of the work suggest that the designer was Sir John's servant, one Thomas Combe. Whatever, a reconstruction of the design in 1981 by the Gladstone Pottery Museum in Longton, Stoke-on-Trent, with the help of students from the North Staffordshire College of Technology, confirmed it to be eminently practicable, although it would be of limited use without a supply of running water and an efficient sewage disposal system. There is no evidence that the American slang term, 'john', owes anything to Harington, although the family does have connections with the United States. There is no evidence, either, sadly, that he or Thomas Combe invented the deckchair, the lawnmower, the alarm clock, the whistling kettle, the spin dryer, the pop-up toaster, the hot air balloon, or the bicycle. But I'm sure they could have. Sir John and Lady Harington may have been early adopters of tea; I cannot say. Raleigh did not begin making bikes until 1885.

Sir John's efforts to raise funds for the rebuilding of Bath Abbey are well attested, but I have taken a liberty in accusing him of inventing Bishop King's dream, even though his is the first mention of it. Still, I feel sure he would have liked the joke. And that he would forgive me for amending some of his words slightly to make them easier for a modern audience, and me.

Sir John began to build his manor-house at Kelston in 1587, after a design of Barozzio of Vignola, an Italian architect of the time and author of a Treatise on the Five Orders of Architecture. An exquisite miniature gold font, the Queen's christening gift, disappeared during the Civil War, when the old mansion suffered repeatedly, 'being alternately plundered by the royalists or Parliamentarians as often as their forces passed that way; but its venerable head still continued to brave the storms of fortune, and the changes and chances of human affairs, till modern taste laid its destructive hand upon the fabric, and in the rage of improvement levelled its turrets with the dust.' (A New Guide through Bath, and its Environs, *by Richard Warner, 1811.)*

MARY HARINGTON, Sir John's 'sweet Mall', outlived her husband by more than twenty years, dying in 1634, aged nearly seventy. These are among the lines Sir John wrote to her with the gift of a diamond on the birth of their first child: 'The stone is true as true, and then how much more precious you.'

Kit Harington, who plays Jon Snow in Game of Thrones, *is among their descendants.*

ROBERT DEVEREUX, the second Earl of Essex, born 1565, was a favourite of Elizabeth. He was undone by arrogance, immaturity and a foolish decision to treat with Hugh O'Neill, the Earl of Tyrone, instead of defeating the wily rebel, or freedom fighter, depending on taste, in the field. Essex was tried for defying the Queen's order not to leave Ireland, and executed in 1601 for rising against her; Tyrone continued in serial insurrection and intrigue until his death in exile in Rome in 1616.

Bath Abbey, or The Abbey Church of St Peter and St Paul, is one of the city's finest accomplishments. The building of the Norman abbey by John of Tours has been noted earlier. The present Abbey was initiated by Bishop King, and built by Henry VII's great master masons, William and Robert Vertue, who were also responsible, in varying degree, for St George's Chapel, Windsor, Henry VII's chapel in Westminster Abbey, and King's College Chapel, Cambridge. Their stone fan vaulting at Bath and in these other churches and chapels is one of the great Gothic glories of England. The Abbey is presently engaged in its Footprint Project, which is restoring the floor, shifted by time and the bodies beneath, and installing a heating system which will, pleasingly, employ the hot springs.

Kelston still enjoys a wonderful aspect, sitting under the valley edge and looking across green Somerset fields to the Avon. And there can be no more beautifully set churchyard than that of St Nicholas, with its plaque to Sir John in the boundary wall; just beyond is the field where once his fine house stood, before its turrets were levelled to the dust, nothing remaining. On a sunny, still Easter day, the calm of the centuries was broken only by the bleating of the heirs to the flock he loved so well.

There are more monuments and memorials in Bath Abbey than in any English church other than Westminster Abbey. Bishop Montague's is the biggest. Sir John does not have one.

See:

> *Bath Abbey (bathabbey.org).*
> *St Nicholas Churchyard, Church Road, Kelston.*
> *The Old Crown, Kelston Road, Kelston, BA1 9AQ.*

Read:

Orlando Furioso, *by Ludovico Ariosto, translated by Sir John Harington, 1591, features the adventures of Orlando, or Roland, Charlemagne's great mythic knight, and includes, among much else, a trip to the moon.*

The New Discourse of a Stale Subject, called the Metamorphosis of Ajax, *by Misacmos, 1596.*

The Epigrams of Sir John Harington, *edited by Gerard Kilroy, 2009.*

The Letters and Epigrams of Sir John Harington, *edited by Norman Egbert McClure, 1930.*

A Privvie in Perfection, *by Jonathan Kinghorn, 1986.*

Bardsnest.blogspot.com

Digging Bath

GEORGE ASHWORTH QUITE OFTEN WONDERED WHY he had retired to Bath, especially on winter days, when the cold checked the breath and froze the bones. This was not what he had imagined, on the few occasions he'd thought about what he would do when his service was done. Life, laughter, swagger: that was his thought of Bath, although he'd never been, then.

But Bath's great days were long gone, even in high season; it was some time since the fancy and the fawners and the flush had followed royalty and fashion to the new destinations, the seaside resorts, whose fresh air and salty diversions were so superior to tired old baths, lukewarm spa drinking water, dull dances and such. Victoria's Bath was dowdy Bath, soot-blackened, soporific, stodgy, almost as ignored as when the Romano-British finally faded, except by the not-so-rich and the retired, like George Ashworth.

George Ashworth, late of the Bengal Army of the East India Company. Active service in Burma and

Bhutan, with a diversion to the Crimea, where his cool head and skills as an engineer made him much admired during the Siege of Sevastopol, if not by the top echelons after some blunt words before and after the Valley of Death. Returned to India just in time to find himself in the Indian Mutiny, where he distinguished himself by his courage and, even more so, his understanding of the Sepoy grievance and rage.

'Sapper George' was never going to advance far in the new Indian Army after that, and he finished his service still a colonel, dutiful, influential in the spread of the infant Indian railway, and still inconveniently outspoken, particularly in his interpretation of the Imperial Burden, which he considered rather too self-assumed. It had a lot to do with his background: George was a Company man, educated at its military seminary in Addiscombe, from humble origins in the North of England which would have much hampered his military career in the British Army.

It would have been remarkable if, after all this, George had not been a touch, how shall we say, *chippy*. Fortunately, though, he was from the gentler side of the Pennines, and so able to laugh at himself, occasionally.

But he was still at something of a loss to explain why he had come to Bath. Swagger and society were not things he necessarily enjoyed; while not exactly a blunt soldier, he was hardly a smooth boulevardier, either. Salons and chips are not always good companions. But he recognised his need of polish, and always hoped it might rub off on him if he put himself in a good strategic position. And then there was the matter of the wife he had been waiting to find for forty years and had half-examined hopes of finally discovering now. Indeed; George, slightly incongruously, was an admirer of Jane Austen, who had been a tremendous help in whiling away a tedious spell up country in Nagaland.

It had been a year now, in his modest house in the modest street beyond Pulteney Bridge and close by Sydney Gardens, and as yet there was no sign of a mature Elizabeth or Anne, nor even an Emma. His social round, such as it was, had speedily proved stultifying. He disliked cards, mostly because he disapproved of luck. Conversation was so safe that no one, apart from him, dared mention any war that the Empire had lost, including the most recent, the first scrap with Boers. Widows with meaningful looks warned widows with pursed lips against Sapper George: 'Not quite like us. Albert/Edward/Henry always said he went native during the Mutiny, protested against the entirely necessary disciplinary action of strapping sepoys across the mouths of cannons and firing. Not sound'.

He had found a small circle of friends: a couple of other old India hands, rather too settled into retirement for George's taste; his doctor, another Austenite happy to have found something to talk about other than elderly ailments; and a few of the more spritely local worthies, including Isaac, a Bath businessman of singular innovation and intellect who enjoyed beating George at chess and arguing with him about religion without trying to convert the sceptical colonel or raising his voice above the soft local tones. Mostly, though, George passed his time reading

Jane and walking through Sydney Gardens, enjoying the trains rumbling along Brunel's exciting cut through to Bath's station. This had become quite the tourist attraction, and it amused him that the vast majority of spectators who assembled to watch were men. He had attempted to discuss this at a stodgy Bath tea, with reference to power and thrust and puffing, and was never invited again. On this particular day, as he was staring at the steam and the hissing machine and missing the mad drama of Howrah railway station, he heard a voice that shouted above the noise, 'Progress, eh?' Turning, he saw he was being addressed by a tall woman of a similar age to him, although substantially less touched by time. Or by any conventional feminine artifice: her hair, grey as nature intended, was piled into a bun; her face was free of adornment bar a pair of sensible spectacles; and she was wearing a sensible tweed suit and shoes. But there was something about the cut – and thrust – of the white blouse beneath that George found unusually unsettling, in a good way.

Even so, unaccustomed to being hailed by a handsome woman unknown to him, he merely smiled a tight smile and reverted to staring in front of him, which made him feel ridiculous. The woman, either oblivious or indifferent to his embarrassment, repeated the remark with the same challenge in her voice. George, after a brief internal battle with indignation and self-consciousness, determined not to be so silly, touched his hat and managed a strangulated but assenting, 'Indeed.'

'What I mean to say,' said the woman, 'is that although we are undoubtedly making progress in many material ways, with these steaming great machines and factories and mills and mines, and in some social ways, including the abolition of slavery and regulation of child labour, there is one important matter which still requires urgent attention.'

George, rallying, fancied he saw his chance. 'I agree, Madam. The army is undoubtedly in need of reform.'

'The army? The army! Unless you are proposing that women should be allowed to join, Sir, I fear your priorities are sadly awry!'

'Women? Join the army! Not a bad idea, actually, Madam, considering what I've seen some men do.'

The woman, taken aback, relaxed into a smile. 'Good gracious. A soldier with an open mind. Where did they keep you?'

'Away, mostly. George Ashworth, late Indian Army.'

'Well. I'm Grace Walmsley, late arrival in the fight for women's equality. Should I call you by your rank? Field Marshal?'

'Happily, I was only a colonel. Call me George.'

George was already finding his new acquaintance more stimulating than almost anyone else – male or female – that he'd met in Bath. He was vaguely aware of women's campaigners, but this was the first he'd come across since returning from India, where, for understandable reasons, they were as scarce as a general able to read a map.

Grace, who, George noticed, had a particularly attractive smile, was much less in thrall to the dreary niceties he found so tedious in Bath. Within minutes, as they walked back through the park, George learnt that she was recently widowed, that her husband, Percy, had been a nice but dull doctor, that she had no children, and that she had now taken up archaeology.

'Ah, yes, digging and things. I was an engineer.'

'No, things and digging, the things are more important than the digging, although you should see my trowel action.'

'So it is with engineering, as the late Mr Brunel would have told you. Where might I be able to observe your way with a trowel? Egypt, Mesopotamia, Troy?'

'Bath, actually.'

'Bath? You mean exciting things do happen here? Where?'

'Near the Pump Room. Major Davis, the City Architect, is in charge. We think we might have found the great bath of Aquae Sulis, buried these last 1500 years.'

'The very bath built by old King Bladud?'

'Bladud? Pshaw, just a myth. They say he tried to fly. Pigs are more likely. No, this is Roman, all right.'

'Will there be gold?'

'Ah, yes, soldier, engineer, man, basic. Probably not, but there's knowledge down there.'

'And just the thing to bring the visitors back and wake this dreary old place up. I was getting fed up trainspotting.'

'Really, George, you mustn't be so inconsistent. A colonel is supposed to like things just the way they are. You'll be telling me you're in favour of votes for women next.'

'Actually, I am. See my earlier reason viz the army. I think every adult in the country should have the vote, man, woman, property owner, non-property owner, tinker, tailor, soldier, widow, archaeologist, retired engineer. When can I come and examine your diggings?'

'Steady, George. I think you should know that I'm not going to marry you.'

George gave a start, and was blushing like a young boy straight from the country before he realised Grace was teasing him, her open and winsome smile containing just the right amount of challenge to an old soldier.

'Sorry, George, obviously startled you a bit. People do find my approach – and my sense of humour – a little too direct at times. Anyway, marriage. Did it once, had enough. Not so much the institutional inequality, but rather the endless routine of it, the charming little idiosyncrasies, the phrases and sayings that become major irritations simply through numbing repetition. "Very tasty," at every meal, for example, or "Steady the Buffs", or "Mustn't grumble", the tuneless whistling, humming and singing the same phrases of songs, "Down at the Old Bull and Bush", "Boiled Beef and Carrots", the calling me "Old girl", the fingers drumming on the table, the same old jokes… Children might have helped, but that didn't happen, either.'

'Poor old Percy. Couldn't he do anything right?'

'Yes, that was a bit harsh. He was kindly, he had excellent manners, and had been quite passably good looking when he was younger. And he got me into archaeology, as it happens. Major Davis was a patient who became a friend after Percy prescribed him a powerful liniment which helped his bad back caused by bending double in excavations. I took a bottle down to him during his initial work on the Roman baths. The smell and thrill of the past, of the earth and stone, damp and warm, the thought of what might be down there still, after all these years, in the dark silence – I thought it was marvellous, still do. Major Davis – Charles – let me help, and I've been digging and scraping ever since. Come and have a look tomorrow.'

They had arrived by the old Sydney Hotel, now a school and shadow of its great days, when it was the entrance to the pleasure gardens, with an orchestra playing from a first floor balcony for the candlelit dances and entertainments, the Cascade and the Cosmorama, mechanical tableaux of cascading water, falling figures, cunning optical illusions of famous scenes from history, the life-sized puppet hermit, the health-giving swings and more, all gone and ghosts now while Bath waited for its revival. George agreed to go down to the dig the next day, and made the short walk to his home with as much spring in his step as was possible for a retired colonel.

*

THE NEXT DAY DISCOVERED GEORGE OUTSIDE THE mighty new Grand Pump Room Hotel, which carried much of Bath's hopes for restored trade and glory. Grace, in the same sensible but really rather alluring tweeds, was in the company of a tall, stooping, bright-eyed man of middling age with an untidy collection of rolled plans in one hand and a pipe in the other. A large and fairly well-behaved deerhound sat next to him. Grace, pleasingly, seemed most pleased to see George.

'Colonel! Prepare to visit the most exciting place in Bath! This is Major Davis, City Architect and Excavator General. Major Davis, Colonel Ashworth. Oh, and this is the Major's dog, Alderman.'

'Ha! Outranked! By a long way as it happens, Colonel. Only Bath Volunteer Rifles and the Worcestershire Militia, I'm afraid, but I find Major instils some respect into the dunderhead dignitaries I have to work with in this city.' He gestured at his dog. 'That's why he's called Alderman. I find it quite therapeutic to give him orders. Down, Alderman! Heel, Alderman!'

The major, apparently oblivious to the attention he was attracting, waved his pipe at the excited Victorian version of Georgian elegance that was the Grand Pump Room Hotel. 'What do you think of that?'

'Well,' said George. 'It's grand.'

'Damned monstrosity. Ghastly mixture of timid and brash. My design was immeasurably better, but the scheming, cheese-paring and envious third-raters here wouldn't wear it. Grubbing away behind the scenes as usual, accusing me of having an unfair advantage by organising the competition to design it and entering one myself, then complaining about the cost. The cheek of it! The sheer brass neck! And the lack of taste! Landed us with that. Ninnies and nincompoops, all of them. Nowhere near full, and when it is full, the acclaimed baths on the ground floor will be nowhere big enough. The amazing Grace says you're an engineer?'

George had just enough time to allow this to be the case before the major plunged on.

'Good, need a bit of sapper input. I've been scratching around here for years, doing what I can while the idiot people and third-raters in charge of this city grumble and mumble about dust and disturbance and keeping their precious visitors away.' The major now gestured over at the Pump Room, which, judging by numbers, was doing desultory business. 'I know there's a huge and pretty much intact Roman bath under there. I uncovered a corner of it ten years ago, but I had to cover it up because the city didn't own the old Kingston bath above part of it and there was the usual fussing and bussing from the third raters about their third rate buildings. But now we do, and I'm having another go. Care to come down?'

'I'd be delighted. I had some experience of tunnelling during the siege of Sevastopol. We thought we might be able to get under the walls but the Russians dug their own tunnels to intercept ours. Something of a mess, frankly, but I was rather proud of my tunnels.'

'Excellent! This is very promising. Follow me. Grace?'

The trio made their way round to Abbey Passage, where there was a large hole. Ordering his dog – 'Sit down, Alderman, stay here and do nothing, as usual!' – the major climbed down a ladder about twenty feet and waited for George and Grace to join him before moving down the tunnel that hadn't at all helped his stoop. They walked for some distance by the light of a Davy lamp, occasionally passing through older transverse tunnels thought to be medieval which there had not yet been time to explore. The sound of picks on stone grew louder and it grew warmer and warmer from the hot springs, water from which was trickling beneath them, creating a heavy, muggy atmosphere. 'We're now under the Pump Room,' said Grace; it amused George to think that all the tedious clinking decorum was proceeding oblivious above them. They moved on further then came to an exposed piece of Roman wall.

'This is the wall they built to enclose the reservoir feeding off the springs,' said the major.

The tunnel now turned to the west, exposing yet more wall. 'Ye gods!' cried George, thrilled by the smell and sight of dust and old mortar in the way only a retired colonel of Sappers could be. 'I knew these people were remarkable engineers, but nothing matches being down here and seeing exactly what they were up to. Amazing! Simply amazing! Do you know, I've not been so excited since we bridged the Manipur near Champhai! But this must have been a simply enormous place!'

'Yes, indeed,' said the major. 'And it's the size that's giving us problems. Look up there – those are the footings of the buildings above us. The city wouldn't be at all amused if the Pump Room suddenly disappeared. But it's a mighty task, bringing in props and supports.'

George pointed to some enormous stone blocks revealed by the digging. 'Why not cut those to size down here and use them to prop up the footings?'

'Very good, Colonel! You said he seemed too imaginative to be a soldier, Grace. Now come and look at the next snag.'

They carried on along the wall and eventually came upon the major's navvies, Irish and sweating heavily in the heat to a man. 'Time for a break, chaps,' shouted the major. The men downed their picks and turned to look at the arrivals.

One immediately approached George. 'Colonel George, Sir, do you remember me? Private Killeen.'

'Killeen! Of course I remember you! How are you? What on earth are you doing here? The last time I saw you, you were, now let me see, ah, yes, that's right, you were taking some buckshee ease in the regimental bazaar at Shivaji Nagar!'

'Ah, Sir, time expired, like you. Shipped out. Not much difference between digging trenches in Secunderabad and digging tunnels here. The heat's about the same. It's the cold out on the railways in all weathers that I'm not so keen on. Too much like Limerick on one of its milder days. Quite a few of the other men here are ex-Indiers, too. You, Sir?'

'Retired to Bath. Touch dull. Fascinating down here, though, isn't it?'

Killeen lowered his voice in the skilled way of the private soldier. 'If you've time to stare, Sir. The major keeps us at it. Miss Grace is a charmer, though, isn't she?'

George lowered his voice in the less skilled way of the officer. 'She certainly is.' He found he was blushing, for the second time in two days and thirty years, and moved on quickly to safer ground. 'You do have to hand it to the Romans. They really were quite remarkable.'

'Indeed they were. I thank the Lady Mary they never got to Ireland or there wouldn't be whimsy or a winding road left.'

The major was looking at where the men had been working. They had just uncovered an arch filled with even larger blocks of Roman masonry. 'This has got to be the outfall from the great bath. I'm not sure how we're going to get through, though. Colonel?'

'I see what you mean. Explosives are the obvious answer, but they might rattle the teacups up there. Perhaps a spoil tunnel? Or another shaft?'

Grace had joined them. 'Why not just go round to the other side and dig down from the King's Bath?'

The silence that followed this was broken by Killeen: 'Brilliant, Miss Grace!'

*

IT SHOULD BE SAID THAT THE MAJOR AND THE COLONEL took this input from Grace with good, well, yes, grace, all things considered and after another pause filled with serious male nodding, frowning and pensive noises made by tongues sucking the back of teeth. The major was a difficult man, but his prejudices were against people who were so stupid as to disagree with him, not people of whatever persuasion who came up with interesting ideas. George was miffed that he had not come up with the plan, but wondered at himself that he was not nearly as miffed as he might have been. Clearly, Killeen had made more than one good point. George realised, rather to his astonishment, and with a smile at Grace, that he was, remarkably, deliciously, wonderfully, and, yes, luckily, in love.

At the major's invitation, they retraced their way out of the tunnel and walked over to the King's Bath. On the way, George was being a little shy with Grace, who put it down to his nose – quite a distinguished nose, she thought – being put out of joint by her idea. In any case, she was too busy telling him about what she quaintly described as the crystal ceiling that was inhibiting women's equality. For his part, the major was becoming increasingly excited about the accelerated imminence of the discovery of the Great Bath: 'This will show them! We'll prove it by Christmas!'

The King's Bath was as sulphurous and steaming as ever; the old statue of King Bladud still presided from its niche; but Victorian decorum had damped down the happy ribald mayhem of former times. Students of prudery noted that nude bathing had been prohibited in 1737 (by Beau Nash), and the mixed variety not long after. Most of the spa users now were enjoying, if that is the correct term, warm water being directed at their vital parts from a great height or multiple orifices in the private needle douches and Berthollet treatments imported from continental spas. The Bath's sparse numbers were being entertained, if that is also the correct term, by the detached and moth-eaten members of a string quartet which looked as if it might have been given its big break by Bladud. The viola player, shaped a little like a quaver, was dealing with a persistent itch on his noise which was a challenge even for Mozart. The major looked down from the viewing gallery and confided in as *sotto* his *voce* got that it would be no consequence to drain the bath so they could get digging. He proposed they should return to his chambers to draw up the scheme for excavation.

The major's office was an arresting sight, decorated as it was in a random fashion with an astonishing array of Roman pottery, coins, and fragments of statuary. 'All from down there,' said Grace. She pointed to a small, damaged but exquisitely sculpted stone sphinx: 'I found that. Isn't it marvellous? Interesting, too, how the sex of the sphinx has always been interchangeable, as if, contrary to the entire history of European civilisation, that is not the important thing.' George was enchanted. Grace was delighted with him, if perhaps a little disappointed not to be challenged.

Unsurprisingly, George began to spend much of his time down at the Baths. The King's Bath had now been drained, the council compliant with the major's demands in the hope of more finds attracting more visitors to its struggling resort. All the same, the major was still being pretty *sotto* about his leading vision, which was to excavate and put on display the Great Bath in all its imperial glory. His worry, as he explained to George and Grace, was that not everyone in Bath would be delighted with an open site next to the Abbey, not least the 'third rate' residents and shopkeepers of the houses and buildings that would have to be demolished to allow the bath to reappear after its dark centuries.

The wisdom of this approach was amply demonstrated when, as they were digging up the floor of the bath, two men appeared at its side. One was tall, the other small, but they shared the furtive air and tight suits most closely associated with members of occupations that seek advantage through other means than endeavour. 'Major Davis?' enquired the smaller man. George, who was now dressed, rather daringly, he imagined, like Killeen and the rest of the navvies, save for a silk neckerchief, indicated the major. 'Might we introduce ourselves? I am Mr Grabbe, and this is my esteemed colleague, Mr Darke. We are instructed by our Client, a man of distinction and influence who prefers to conduct his business through the intercession of others and under the cloak of modest anonymity. Could I just lower my voice, Major, and allude to Someone of Importance with Many Interests in This City although he does not necessarily hail from within its boundaries nor even those of this proud country of ours. Isn't that right, Mr Darke?' The taller man nodded solemnly but said nothing.

'Good God!' exclaimed the major. 'Get to the point or we'll be here another 2,000 years.'

'Certainly, Major. Forgive me; I had forgotten that you are a man of action. Let me come, without further ado, circumlocution or what the vulgar among us term "fuss", to the point. My Client has views which he wishes to communicate to you regarding the current works here and your future intentions, views which we are certain you will find persuasive. Is there somewhere more suitable to such a discussion? We need not detain your head navvy, and the matter will be a little complicated for your mother. Isn't that the correct approach, Mr Darke?' The silent partner nodded again, with a mouth particularly downturned to express the gravity of the matter.

The two indicated were, of course, George and Grace. George smiled, but Grace was not amused. 'Charles, let me give you the benefit of the experience gained over my vast years. First, beware of all men, but particularly those in tight suits who have difficulty speaking plainly. Second, speaking plainly, do not talk to the monkeys, talk to the organ grinder.'

The major clapped his hands in delight. 'Wonderful! Gentlemen, this is not my mother, this is the very talented archaeologist, Mrs Grace Walmsley. Second, if your client or whatever you want to call him has matters of importance to communicate to me, he will have to do it in person, and in the presence of my two chief advisors, Mrs Walmsley and this gentleman, who is the distinguished soldier, Colonel George Ashworth.'

Mr Darke's mouth became even more downturned, while Mr Grabbe betrayed some agitation. 'I'm not sure that would be possible, Major Davis. My Client is a person of maximum discretion who is rarely seen in public and who would not want to advertise his Interest and Interests.'

Grace, still indignant for at least two reasons, interjected before the major had chance to reply, 'Well, then, we have just the place. Private, discreet, dimly lit, with no possibility of being disturbed. If your chief, employer, international man of mystery or whatever he is wants to meet us he should come down our tunnel in Abbey Passage at dusk tomorrow evening, with or without you two. A Davy lamp would be useful but he will not need an overcoat.'

*

THE NEXT EVENING, THE MAJOR, THE COLONEL AND GRACE saw a flickering light approaching them along the tunnel. Rather to their surprise, a note had been dropped round to the major's chambers earlier in the day to confirm the appointment: 'Esteemed Major, our Client, despite being a very Important man with many Commitments, Interests and Other Calls on his Very Valuable Time, will meet you in the appointed place this evening at six of the clock. We are your Exceedingly Humble servants, E Grabbe, Esq. & S Darke, Esq (Hon.).' The major had been all for ignoring the appointment, but the colonel and Grace were eager to discover more of the mysterious client.

'This is really quite exciting, and quite un-Bath,' George had said. 'Reminds me of undercover work in the old market at Thimphu. Very Kipling if not very productive. But there is one precaution I will take for which we might be very grateful.' He laid a finger along his distinguished nose and said no more; he was enjoying being both secretive and decisive, particularly as Grace was so obviously impressed.

The light arrived to reveal Mr Darke leading Mr Grabbe and their client. He was a large man with a trace of a foreign accent and hair of a vividly unnatural hue styled with great elaboration. Mr Grabbe effected the introductions, referring to his client as that and no more. The Client came forward and addressed the major: 'Slightly aggressive dog you've got up there, Major, but open to the bribe of a half-eaten Bath Oliver, eh, Darke?' Mr Darke nodded, holding one hand gingerly in the other.

'But let's get down to business,' said the Client. 'Great tunnel you have here, Major, a great tunnel. Actually, it's a great project you have here, great project. I'm a great admirer of the past, great admirer. The past is beautiful. So beautiful. In fact I've lived in it a lot, great place. But so is the future. And there is more money to be made out of it.'

It was clear, even in the flickering light of the lamps, that the major, predictably, was becoming restive, but the Client continued with the confidence of a man accustomed to an audience, emphasising each point with a gesture of his right hand, which, like his left, was small. 'Let me explain my position clearly and with no room for doubt, no room for any doubt. Doubt is bad. So bad. I like Bath. I love Bath. Great place, great people. Some of the best people in the world. But no one can deny it's not what it was. Not at all. And this is where I come in. I want to make Bath great again. And how am I going to do this? I'm going to build a great–' Here he was interrupted by a sudden sneeze from Mr Darke, which he followed by producing a large handkerchief and blowing into it in a loud and prolonged manner.

'Apologies, apologies, one and all,' said Mr Grabbe. 'Mr Darke suffers terribly with his sinuses and the atmosphere down here, if you'll forgive me, Major, is quite oppressive.'

The major made one of his impatient gestures, and the Client, who had remained impassive during the interruption, continued, 'I am going to build a great hotel. A hotel that will draw visitors from far and wide. Wide and far. Wide and wide, far and far. Not a hotel like the Grand Pump Room Hotel. Have you seen that hotel? Old-fashioned, out-dated, with a terrible offer. Terrible.'

'Well at least we can agree on that,' said the major.

'Wait for it,' said Grace.

'And not nearly tall enough. My hotel will be 300 feet high.'

'300 feet!' cried the major. 'Where do you propose to put it?'

'That's the beauty of this beauty of a scheme. Right next to the Abbey. My guests will be able to look down on those funny little angels on their ladders.'

'You swine!' shouted Grace.

'I say!' said George.

The major, for once, was calmer. 'You're more deluded than I thought. I am the City Architect. Such a scheme will proceed over my dead body.'

'I was coming to that. But first let's try to do a deal. I'm a deal-maker. You must know that your hog-eyed plan to excavate the Great Bath and then just leave it there won't impress anybody. Who wants to look at an old ruin? So untidy. The big-wigs in this city won't like it. The people who own the properties you're going to have to pull down won't like it, believe me, and many of them are known personally to me, good people, wonderful people, reasonable people who are going to love my hotel, especially after I've bribed them.

'But I know all about you, Major. I've made it my business to know. You're stubborn, like me. I like that. You're going to fight. I appreciate that. But every man has his price. Name yours.'

'I'm glad you said every man,' said Grace.

The major remained calm, and rather magnificent. 'My price would be you in a cell. I work for the most beautiful, cultured, historic city in the world. I work to make it more beautiful and cultured while preserving and displaying its history. You cannot put a price on that.'

'That's a pity. A great pity. I can't let you get in my way. You shall have to be removed, permanently.'

'Are you proposing to force me into an early retirement or an early grave? This is Bath!'

'Difficult to tell the difference, I agree. And what would be the loss of two more old people and one not-so-young person? We could do it right here. Three more skeletons to join the rest of these Roman folks lying about. Mr Grabbe and Mr Darke are most proficient in the art of dispatch. Their enquiries have shown that you two old people don't have any relatives, and most people would just be relieved to get rid of you, Major.'

'You are a barbarian,' said Grace. 'The barbarians finished off Rome and now you want to finish off Bath. But Mr Whoeveryouare, we are not going to let you!'

'Please. You, lady, are really beginning to irritate me. I like the ladies, but only when they know their place, which is accepting my advances with gratitude. It's going to be a pleasure disposing of you.'

George moved in front of Grace. 'Can we be clear? You are attempting to bribe us, and failing that, to murder us so that your ghastly hotel can be built?'

'You're a little slow on the uptake, aren't you, Colonel? No wonder your army has been in retreat for years. Yes, that's right. So right. As you're not going to be reasonable and accept my bribes, Mr Grabbe and Mr Darke are going to have to kill you.'

'Isaac!' shouted George. 'You can come out now!'

George's friend Isaac now appeared from around the bend in the tunnel immediately behind the colonel, Grace and the major. In one hand he was carrying a lamp whose light had been concealed by the glare of theirs. In the other, he had a notebook. 'This,' said George, 'is my good friend, Isaac Pitman, celebrated citizen of Bath and inventor of the internationally recognised Pitman system of shorthand. He has a complete record of what you have said, offered and threatened, Sir. Your machinations and nefariousnesses are at an end. In shorthand, if you like, the jig is up!'

'Grabbe, Darke, get them!' shouted the Client, who turned on his heel and made off back up the tunnel surprisingly swiftly for a bulky man. His henchmen were no match for their outraged opponents. Grabbe received a hefty kick from Grace in those parts where men and women are not equal and sank to the floor. Darke, meanwhile, described an interesting arc through the air, precipitated by one of George's favourite throws gleaned from his study and practise of the Mushtiyuddha, the great Indian martial art. He went down heavily, emitting the first sound any of them had heard, 'Aaarrgghhh!', which Isaac faithfully recorded.

The Major had chased after the Client, followed by Grace and George, but, other than some particularly blood-curdling barking from Alderman at the tunnel entrance, there was no sign of him. Nor, when they returned, of Grabbe and Darke (Isaac had been too engrossed reading his note back to notice). They had presumably gone up one of the old tunnels; the Major, after confiding that it was the first time an Alderman had been of any use, gave it as his considered view that they would have to be extremely lucky to find their way out.

Perhaps they were; perhaps they were not: they were certainly never seen again, although Killeen, who became head of works for the city, claimed to hear strange unearthly cries from below the streets from time to time. Nor was Bath troubled further by the Client; but it is surely no coincidence that this was the time when skyscrapers first began to appear across the Atlantic. The Major continued on his rumbustious way. The Great Bath was uncovered, and made acceptable to the sensibilities of Bath's fathers by a scheme eschewing the expense of restoring the roof but adding some tasteful statues. This commission did not go to the Major, who was as incandescent about it as when one of the local shopkeepers successfully sued the City for the disruption to his business caused by the excavations. George and Grace continued to help him, and to fight for electoral reform. They also lived openly in what scandalised parts of Bath (most) liked to term sin; every so often, George would go down, increasingly carefully, on one knee and beg Grace not to marry him, and she would respond happily, 'Never!' The advisability of marriage was his only real disagreement with Miss Austen; but he did like to point out that she, too, had rejected a proposal.

Oh, and the Major did finally get to build his hotel. The Empire Hotel, a very bold statement overlooking the Avon which has divided opinion ever since, not least because it really is rather tall.

Afterword

GEORGE AND GRACE DID NOT EXIST, ALTHOUGH *their careers and characters share similarities with those who did. 'Hellfire Jack' Olpherts, for example, SIR WILLIAM OLPHERTS VC (1822–1902), was a gunner who saw service in both the Crimea and the Indian Mutiny. But it has to be said that he was rather more robust than George: after extolling the virtues of sobriety at a temperance meeting, he concluded by thumping the table and exclaiming that 'he would not give a straw for a soldier who would not take his glass of grog like a man!' EMILY BLATHWAYT, though too young (1852–1940) for these events, was a suffragette who, together with her husband, Lieutenant-Colonel LINLEY BLATHWAYT, late of the British Indian Army, and their daughter, Annie, threw open their house in Batheaston as a refuge for suffragettes recovering from hunger strikes. The house had been owned and re-modelled by John Wood, and also had links with his son. Colonel Blathwayt created an arboretum in the grounds below Solsbury Hill, planting trees to commemorate leading campaigners for women's rights, including Emmeline Pankhurst, Christabel Pankurst, Annie Kenney, Charlotte Despard, Millicent Fawcett and Lady Lytton. The Blathwayts disagreed with the more violent methods of the suffragettes, but continued to support the women's movement. Colonel Blathwayt just lived to see the Reform Bill of 1918 that gave women over thirty the right to vote. Mary Blathwayt lived on in Eagle House until her death in 1961. The grounds were later sold off and the arboretum destroyed to make way for a housing development. One tree out of nearly fifty, an Austrian Pine planted by Rose Lamartine Yates, survives; replacements for the others have been planted in Victoria Park, Alice Park and at Bath Spa University.*

As for George's passion for Miss Austen, debate rages – politely – about whether she can be truly described as a feminist; some doubt has also been cast on the story of her acceptance then refusal twenty-four hours later of the wealthy and delightfully named Harris Bigg-Wither, Esquire, of Manydown Park, Wootton St Lawrence, Hants.

The biographical details about Major CHARLES EDWARD DAVIS (1827–1902) are correct, as is the account of his discovery of the Great Bath, save for the role of George and Grace and Private Killeen. The apparent conflict between his architectural practice and role as the City Architect did result in a series of disputes which saw his competition entries for the Grand Pump Room Hotel and the Great Bath rejected. A local tradesman did sue the Council for the loss caused by the excavations. Criticism at the time that the Major didn't take sufficient care to preserve the Roman remains has been proved unfounded. He was a keen breeder of deerhounds and rarely unaccompanied by one, although the name Alderman is not recorded.

And he did build The Empire, known to some as 'Major Davis's Revenge'. It is well worth a look at, even if Sir Nikolaus Pevsner did call it 'a monstrosity and an unbelievable piece of pompous architecture'. The Major betrays his Victorianism with his representations on the roof of the English class system, with the castle on the corner for the upper classes, the house for the middle classes and a cottage for the lower classes. Whatever, his care for the city certainly contributed to its listing as a UNESCO World Heritage Site in 1987.

Sir ISAAC PITMAN (1813–1897) lived in Bath for fifty-eight years; besides developing his method of shorthand, he was also an enthusiastic vegetarian, teetotaller and follower of the Swedish mystic, Emanuel Swedenborg, whose New Church was founded on his vision that Jesus Christ was the One God and obedience to Christian teachings. Pitman belonged to a thriving New Church community in Bath and printed tracts in its support at his own expense. It was a gentle creed, so doomed not to prevail, although there are still followers in Bath (and, pleasingly, in Bath, Maine). I do not know whether Sir Isaac played chess; but his publishing firm, Sir Isaac Pitman & Sons, was a legendary provider of books on the game.

Any similarities between Silas and Edgar in 'Bath, Oliver?' and Mr E Grabbe and Mr S Darke in this story are entirely intentional.

See:

> *The Roman Baths (romanbaths.co.uk), in addition to its exhibits, sights and attractions, the excellent Roman Baths also organise tours of the old tunnels on selected days.*
>
> *The World Heritage Centre, opened in the former Victorian Spa Buildings, celebrating the City and its ranking by UNESCO as a World Heritage Site (bathworldheritage.org.uk).*
>
> *The Holburne Museum, sited in the old Sydney Hotel in the Sydney Pleasure Gardens is based on the collection of Sir William Holburne (1793–1874), resident of Bath and hero of Trafalgar (holburne.org).*

Read:

> Roman Bath Discovered, *by Barry Cunliffe, 1971.*
>
> Major Davis: Architect and Antiquarian, *by Barry Cunliffe, 1986.*

The Emperor Waiting

THERE. LOOK, OVER THERE: THE SMALL, CLOAKED figure near the Abbey, outside the Pump Room. You might not have noticed him; not everyone does, even though he is followed by a very tall robed figure with two very small dogs on leads.

Let me describe him further. Neatly bearded, dark, he is elegant in his Gieves & Hawkes double-breasted grey suit and his highly polished Lobb's shoes, the cloak an exotic touch. In other men and other places, there might be something laughable about the sight; but he has poise, dignity: an impassive, impressive man with much to be impassive and impressive about.

Who is he, exactly? That is a problem: the exactly. He is not exactly a man, because he has some followers who believe him to be God. Perhaps he is. He himself is not sure. He is sure he is an emperor, even if he doesn't exactly have what you might recognise as an empire, and he doesn't always have even that.

This man is, by turn and opinion, cold, charming,

arrogant, cruel, kindly, selfish, selfless, honourable and devious. Was there ever a king who wasn't so reported? Let alone an emperor: there are, we can at least agree, no humble emperors. And this one has a lineage through time's shifting mists. He is, he and some say, 225th in a direct line from King David, descended from Menelik, the son of Solomon and Sheba, conceived when the Queen came out of Africa bringing the King jewels and gold to exchange for wisdom.

Yes; this is indeed His Imperial Majesty Haile Selassie I, the Negus, King of Kings, Lord of Lords, Conquering Lion of the Tribe of Judah, Elect of God, the Light of the World, The Holiest and Most Mighty Jah Rastafari. And he seems to be in Bath.

In Bath? Really? How? Well, I can give you some facts. But the facts are not the story. They cannot shift the mists. There are not nearly enough of them. And why, when there is more legend, should the facts hold sway?

The Emperor has now paused before the Abbey front and is staring up at the angels climbing their ladders. It would be fine to report that the two little dogs are staring up with him, but they are not; they are wrapping themselves round and round the very tall man who holds their leads. The Emperor likes small dogs. His favourite was called Lulu, who was not so popular with everyone, as he had a habit of misbehaving himself over their shoes, and could not, obviously, be reprimanded. Also, despite or because of being short – he stands five feet and four inches – the Emperor likes tall servants. The tallest was called Balahu; he was over seven feet tall and had two main roles: Imperial Umbrella Carrier of the Lion of Judah and Drum Major of the Imperial Fanfare. But he was shot by the Italians, apparently. This servant is also carrying an umbrella, which is complicated, with the dogs, but wise, in Bath.

Apparently. Allegedly. Perhaps. As I say, plenty of problems here for the taxonomists of time, the fetishists of facts, the enemies of wonder. They will, for example, have nothing of His Imperial Majesty's line of descent, although they cannot disprove it. No one can be certain when and how Jews and Jewry, Christians and Christianity came to the Emperor's country. It is a matter of belief, so why not believe him?

The Emperor's country is another uncertainty, an entwined and proximate collection of lands and peoples lent relish and mystery by their euphony and our ignorance: Axum, Lalibela, Oromo, Shoa, Sidama, Gurage, Wolayta, Dizi, Tigray, Afars, Gurage, Agaw, Harar, Eritrea, all part at times of the shifting entity of no fixed name – Ethiopia? Abyssinia? – just beyond the edge of what was called until rather recently The Known World. This is a realm only fitfully described by travellers' tales of height and colour, made yet more mysterious by the fabled presence of the mighty but elusive Prester John, the Christian king for whom Europe waited for centuries, the dark warrior whose armies would come crusading out of Africa.

I think we can take it that the Prester is not coming now. But don't for a moment think this slick-crass world's writ has run all over the domain of The Light of the World. Not while the Ark of the Covenant is still in Axum. It was brought there 2,500 years ago after the Babylonians sacked Jerusalem and destroyed the Temple of Solomon. It is now kept in a chapel by the Church of Mary of Zion, where no one but the Guardian of the Ark has seen it since the Emperor Iyasus I went inside 300 years ago. The Guardian of the Ark, a monk of the Ethiopian Orthodox Church, is chosen for life by his predecessor and elders. Once chosen, he is forbidden ever to leave the chapel. Ask him for his name, and he will reply, 'I am the Guardian of the Ark. I have no other name'. Ask the Patriarch of the Ethiopian Church if the Ark is there, and he will reply, 'We don't doubt that it is here, in our place. We don't have to prove it to anyone'.

Or to prove that the Emperor is in Bath, where he is now heading towards Parade Gardens. He came here after the Italians invaded his empire in 1936 with rather more success than in 1895, when they were roundly and savagely defeated at the Battle of Adwa. The Emperor is not a military man, although he led his army, fired machine guns and charged the Italians, to no avail, heavy losses and defeat. He had to decide whether to fight on or flee for help from the rest of the world, now unconvincingly come together as the League of Nations. He gave a fine and dignified speech to the League in Geneva that achieved nothing. The British, their own faltering empire faced by the rising rivals of Germany, Italy and Japan, offered him sanctuary but no enthusiasm. His imperial counterpart, the new monarch, Edward VIII, might have been expected to proffer a brotherly hand, but did not.

Indeed, he considered the Emperor to be causing him 'a certain inconvenience'; still, he no doubt had other things on his mind.

It was not like this in 1930, when the King's younger brother, the Duke of Gloucester, travelled to Addis Ababa for the Emperor's coronation, an entrancing composition of ancient and modern, Europe and Africa, gorgeous caparisons and bedecked livery, uniforms tailored in London from lion skins, dancing priests, antiphons, canticles, plainsong, all in the sacred tongue of Ghiz; slumbering chiefs and dozing envoys, prostrating crowds, vigilant machine guns, vigorous three-plane flypast, a royal carriage that had belonged to the Kaiser, and a coachman who had driven Franz Joseph, which would have made him venerable at the least. The Duke of Gloucester brought a coronation cake said to weigh a ton. Evelyn Waugh came to describe it all. No wonder Africa and its downtrodden diasporas saw this stunning reversal in precedence as a sign of a change so significant that numbers of them hailed as their foretold Messiah the man born Ras Tafari.

But was it really like that then? Or now? Europeans and Ethiopians saw what they wanted to see: for some it is easier to smile at the strange and to suspect the ploy, the power-shoring; for others, mystery and awe take claim. Certainly that is what they saw on the newsreels in Harlem, read in Jamaica, when they watched the Duke bow to the Emperor. Enough to make a messianic movement. Enough to excite that hero and villain, according to belief, Marcus Garvey, who had told his followers, 'Look to Africa for a black king'. Enough to bring out crowds of supposedly stolid English when the Emperor arrived in London.

And in Bath, even more so. I might say this had something to do with living on a site venerated as sacred for a few thousand years. You might think this fanciful. I might ask the Emperor, now sitting on a bench in Parade Gardens while his servant walks the little dogs with great dignity. The Emperor would be polite – he is always polite – but he is not a confiding man. He does seem to like the order of English parks, and the English seaside. He has sat, familiarly impassive, in Worthing, Weston-super-Mare, Burnham-on-Sea, Brighton and elsewhere, pondering his fate or simply taken by that familiar urge to study the horizon as if somehow it were the future.

Bath, though. Why? Well, the Emperor is not the man to say. He was not entirely welcome – convenient – in London. Perhaps he was looking for somewhere, something – anything – familiar, and was suited by an ancient place with as laden and significant a past as his. Perhaps that was what he sensed amid the Roman traces and John Wood's druid fancies adorning the stone crescent and circus, sun and moon. Perhaps he takes some small solace in being so welcomed to the city of the forebears his invaders are trying so hard to emulate. Details make for ease, too: difficult, in Bath, not to notice the lions in stone, more than fifty of them, a familiar thing for the Emperor; the Lion of Judah, to whom all the lions in Ethiopia belong, including the pair he presented to the King Emperor George V on his first visit to Britain, much good it did him. Including too, the ones that guarded his palace in Addis Ababa and were said to have been shot by the invading Italians; and the ones said to have been shot by the Emperor for failing to guard against another coup. It can be dangerous, being a symbol. King Edgar the Peaceful, crowned at Bath in 973, when the Emperor Mara Takla Haymanot ruled in Ethiopia, was the first English king to choose the lion as his symbol. His coronation was a great event. He was also a small man, as it happens. But he kept invaders out, and died in his bed.

In Bath, to Bath, the Emperor appears a man of reserve and presence, preserving dignity in defeat, projecting a hope he might not feel, provoking sympathy for his plight. But that is not all of him. It would be a mistake to think of him as some impotent time-overtaken toy, a kind of African Windsor. Whatever else he might be, he is not stupid. Emperors in Ethiopia do not become Emperors in Ethiopia by anything as simple and unsophisticated as primogeniture. He is not the son of the Emperor Menelik II, hero of Adwa, but a nephew. He has always been patient; he worked and waited to become Emperor for twenty years, from his appointment as Governor of Harar when he was eighteen to his coronation in 1930. In between were a curtailed reign by an emperor and a longer reign by an empress during which the then Ras Tafari was crown prince, regent and de facto ruler. These events and successions were not seamlessly accomplished, but rather accompanied by a swirling, serpentine mix of conspiracy, plot, insurrection and deposition involving royal relations, bodyguards and rival warlords whose only constant was his surviving influence. It would perhaps be naive to enquire too deeply into the Emperor's methods; specifically to wonder about the mysterious death in 1935 of his deposed predecessor as the Italians arrived. As well ask his Roman imperial peers about their interesting methods and outcomes.

Let us just say that such a life prompts a liking for high walls as well as patience. The Emperor chooses not to live in a fine Bath terrace, but in a Victorian mansion a little way out in Weston, with grounds and said walls. The irony of the house's Italianate style has not escaped him. He has the Empress Menen with him, some of the time, when she can stand the English climate, and five of his children and five grandchildren. It is not surprising he likes to take a walk, to be alone with the future he is convinced he has, but not always.

Twilight is turning to dusk. In Parade Gardens, some interesting figures can also be seen, nearing, locked in lively conversation, overcoated against the Bath summer. One of them, slightly detached, notices the Emperor and comes to join him. This is Gaius Suetonius Paulinus, Governor of Britain. He nods at the servant, now returned, and makes a fuss of the small dogs before joining the Emperor on his bench. 'Good evening, Your Imperial Majesty. I trust you don't mind me joining you; I'm finding my comrades and superiors even more trying than usual today. Caesar is banging on about Gaul yet again. I expect you know it's divided into three parts? Claudius's stutter is particularly pronounced, and Hadrian's obsession with his wall is becoming remarkably wearing. Agricola, Scapula and I have argued with him until we're as blue in the face as a Briton that the way to keep these tediously aggressive barbarians down is a brisk punitive expedition, not skulking behind a wall. What is it about rulers and walls? As I may have told you before, all three of us had great success as governors giving Scots, Picts, Iceni, you name it, a vigorous biffing at all times of revolt and restiveness. And don't get me started on Constantine: has that man ever been wrong about anything? Spent some time in Yorkshire, of course, and you don't have to be on this island very long to know what that means. And how are you, Sir? Any news on your return?'

The more alert of those of you who have visited the Roman baths will have realised by now that this distinguished gathering is normally in place on plinths around the Great Bath. But not always. Suetonius, a stocky, energetic figure, has placed his splendid helmet on the bench and is now making vigorous imaginary sword thrusts in front of him as he sits. The Emperor, as is usual, smiles and says nothing.

'Don't be discouraged, that's the thing. Your invaders talk of a new Roman empire but they're really not up to it. Caesar's not at all impressed by their stubby posturing leader, reminds him of a marginally more sane Caligula, says he'll be overthrown and upended, literally – and Caesar is a literary man, as he never stops telling us. Their army isn't fit to lace the sandals of our mighty legions. No stamina, none of the drilled self-belief that makes you fight to the last man far from your hearth, overwhelmed by vicious strangers and strangeness. Oh, I know it all went a bit soft in the end, but in my day what a force we were! We had formidable opponents here, too. I don't mean the druids, feeble bunch of incanters and imprecators, imagined that standing in a circle, waving their arms around and chanting would be very much use against my boys in the XIV. Quite a bit of slaughter, but no regrets, as they had some very nasty habits. Anglesey's rather nice now, they tell me. No, when I talk formidable, I'm talking about Boudicca: what a warrior! A damn close run thing, as someone said, and the Brits still managed their usual trick of turning her defeat into some kind of triumph. Believe the legend, too: she is buried under Platform 10 of King's Cross station, although of course it wasn't there in those days.

'You'll be all right. The Brits are going to want you back *in officio*. They've got good instincts, fundamentally, a terrific sense of self-preservation, and a gift for the unorthodox, if not the downright sneaky. It's an unbeatable combination. Don't make the mistake of trusting them: identify their interests and play to them. We can see great things coming. Great things. Never pays to look too far ahead, though. I'm a bit of an old Africa hand myself, you know. First man to take troops over the Atlas Mountains, hell of a march, what heat, fry an egg on my shield, we started out from Mauretania in July, tell a lie, August–'

Suetonius is interrupted by an imperious shout; he leaves hurriedly to join his companions, adjusting his helmet as he goes, grumbling in a soldierly way. The Emperor watches them until they disappear. Then he retraces his steps, thoughtful as ever, past the Abbey (another contemplation of the angels), past the Baths, up Milsom Street, round Queen Square, and up to Victoria Park, named for a princess who also became imperial. As he passes, the two fine bronze lions guarding the gate from Queen's Parade rise in salute. The little dogs slink past. The park is now closed to ordinary mortals, but nobody sees the Emperor, who stops to smell the lilies, so profuse in his faraway palace gardens, and then keeps carrying on.

Afterword

HAILE SELASSIE RETURNED TO AFRICA FROM ENGLAND
*in 1940, after Mussolini declared war on Britain and
France, abruptly curtailing a passage of futile appeasement
and necessitating the ousting of Italy from Ethiopia and its
African colonies. The Emperor was escorted clandestinely
to Khartoum, the capital of Sudan, then a British colony in
all but name, where he was given the surely unconvincing
soubriquet of 'Mr Smith' while an invasion of Ethiopia was
got underway.*

*It was an outdated, sepia sort of affair, a last rally of
empires that would not long survive, although few would
have predicted the Emperor's would last longest; one of
the last campaigns, too, which could be considered at all
romantic, if that can ever be allowed of war.*

*British, Indian, Kenyan, Sudanese, South African,
Rhodesian and even Palestinian soldiers formed the
British forces attacking from the two fronts of Sudan
and Kenya. The army from Sudan was commanded by
the Kaid, the Egyptian title for a governor, in reality the*

rather less euphonious Major General Platt.

The campaign also featured a cast of characters unequalled even in the headiest days of irregular imperial heroes:

Laurens van der Post, Captain, South African Bloomsbury protege and anthropologist, later guru to the Prince of Wales, part of the special forces thrust which took the Emperor back into his country accompanied by two Persian rugs to lend his tent a little dignity.

Wilfred Thesiger, Captain, legendary explorer of the Arabian Empty Quarter, who was awarded the DSO after marching fifty miles in twenty-four hours to cut off and force the surrender of a far superior force of 8,000 Italians.

Hugh Boustead, Lieutenant-Colonel, who had deserted from the Royal Navy in the First World War to fight in France, where he won an MC, then fought with the White Russians, captained the British Olympic Pentathlon team, and joined the Fourth Everest expedition before becoming District Commissioner for Darfur.

George Steer, Captain, Spectator *writer, Special Operations officer, old acquaintance of the Emperor and inspired propagandist, who pioneered megaphone messages encouraging desertion and carried a leaflet printing press with him.*

Daniel Sandford, Brigadier, DSO, animal skin trader, farmer, special forces operative and

Chief Political Adviser to the Emperor.

Arnold Weinholt, Etonian, lion hunter, Australian rancher and senator, Boer War officer, over sixty, killed in an ambush. Thesiger watched him go off on his last mission, hauntingly, like some Rider Haggard hero, with 'gun on shoulder, stick in hand, starting with his donkeys on his last journey into the interior'.

And if that wasn't enough peculiarly Anglo-eccentricity, the leader of the special force, which he called Gideon after the Bible prophet and guerrilla fighter, was none other than Orde Wingate, the almost certainly certifiable but inspired Zionist, jungle fighter and war hero, who addressed the Emperor thus on their first meeting, in Khartoum: 'Now that the lot has fallen to me in a fair ground, I will with God's help be an instrument to set right a great wrong. I pledge my life to restore Your Majesty to your rightful throne and ask only in return that you trust and support me absolutely.'

What chance did the varyingly enthusiastic forces of Italian fascism have against this assembly? The conventional armies of Platt and Cunningham might have been more practically responsible for victory, but the Emperor and his irregulars lived the legend. Haile Selassie re-entered Addis Ababa on May 5, 1941 in triumph and remained Emperor for another thirty-three years.

(Wingate, after a failed attempt to stab himself to death while depressed, went on to form the legendary Chindits, the long-range guerrilla groups, whose achievements are viewed either as a real disruption of Japanese operations in

Burma or marvellous morale-boosting propaganda. What cannot be questioned is the hardship and heroism. Their leader's subsequent career and attendant eccentricities – the nudity, the wearing of onions and garlic round his neck to ward off mosquitoes – was cut short by a plane crash in north-east India in 1944.)

In 1954, Haile Selassie returned to Britain on a state visit, receiving the invitation to dine at Buckingham Palace that had eluded him earlier. He made a special trip to Bath to be made a Freeman of the City, greeted once again by large crowds attracted to this early example of a twentieth-century celebrity.

He became increasingly feted as a world leader in the new order that evolved after the Second World War, courted by both sides of the Cold War, travelling widely, leading African opinion and calls for development. But there was always an essential contradiction between the supposed moderniser and the Emperor who was hailed as the living god of Rastafari when he visited Jamaica in 1966.

He was ambivalent about that, as about so much else; the Emperor is a leading example of that old and ticklish bind for absolute monarchs, how to reconcile progress with privilege, how to relinquish power, but not too much. And so there was talk of new factories and machines, of modernisation and destiny while the people went without fair trial and food and the Emperor was in his palace, surrounded by self-serving servants, keeping implacable reality at bay by clinging to flattering antique protocols and working obsessively at anything other than the reforms that might have saved him.

That is the current view, and may be harsh. But in the end – and it had to end – Haile Selasse was overthrown and imprisoned in 1974 by the Derg, a Marxist-inspired movement led by army officers and fuelled by a famine widespread and ignored until revealed by a British television programme. But, as with the rest of him, the unknown and the oblique remain: his death is still a mystery, although most have it that he was strangled the next year and secretly buried in his palace under a latrine, a touch surely intended to mar his mystique. In 2000, after a state funeral ordered by a current government currying royalist support, his remains were placed in a great marble tomb in the Holy Trinity Cathedral built, in finest imperial tradition, by him. The Rastafari believe he is not dead, that he cannot die; they say the bones re-buried are not his, that he is preparing his return. And who is to say not?

The Emperor has many descendants; his grandson, Crown Prince Zera Yacob Amha Selassie, educated at Eton and Oxford, lives in Addis Adaba. Unsurprisingly, given everything else, a great-nephew has written a book about German manners.

Haile Selassie gave Fairfield House, his home in Bath, to the people of Bath. Today it is the home of the Bath Ethnic Minorities Senior Citizens' Association, and hosts a remarkable mixture of culture and religion in fine and fitting tribute to the Emperor's eclectic internationalism, tolerances, interests and constructive ambiguities. Rastafarian and Ethiopian Orthodox revered objects and artefacts are on display along with photographs and mementos of Haile Selassie's time in Bath. The curious blend of familiar and strange that surrounds the Emperor is repeatedly pointed up, not least by the photograph of him opening an English church fete four months after charging the Italian army on horseback. There is a prayer room and the studio of Imperial Voice, a radio station dedicated to his message and 'broadcasting goodness to the world'.

When I visited Fairfield House, entering past the sheltered housing of Empress Menen Gardens, I met Methuselah, a Rastafarian, 'forty-eight this lifetime', as he told me with a smile. He said that the Emperor had chosen Fairfield for the view across the valley to the hills, which reminded him of his lost Harar (there are those who say they are nothing like Harar, but this seems quite fitting for the Emperor). Methuselah said Haile Selassie also chose Bath because it, too, had hot springs, much favoured by the Emperor in his own country: Methuselah had visited some, and found them excellent, and cheaper than Bath. Yes, he said, there was still a presence at Fairfield. He had grown up on the other side of the valley; as a boy he used to look across at night and see a light; later he found it came from Fairfield. The Light of the World, then.

The statues of the Roman Emperors most closely associated with Britain and its most noted governors were among the last works of the busy imperial sculptor, George Anderson Lawson. They were commissioned to adorn the winning design for the new Great Bath building which opened in 1897, with one exception:

Julius Caesar is by Lawrence Tindall, replacing Lawson's statue, which was tipped into the Bath by some students in 1989, breaking into three places. Sic Semper Tyrannis, clearly. No one now knows where Suetonius defeated Boudicca; the legend that she is buried under what is now Platform 10 at King's Cross Station is without substantiation but remains remarkably persistent.

See:

> *Fairfield House, Kelston Road, BA1 3QJ (fairfieldhouse.org).*
>
> *The Bath Spa Hotel. The Emperor and his family stayed here when they first came to Bath; there is a fine photo of Haile Selassie in the foyer (macdonaldhotels.co.uk).*
>
> *The Pump Room lobby displays a striking photo of the Emperor in Bath (romanbaths.co.uk).*
>
> *The Little Theatre, St Michael's Place, BA1 1SG, has a Haile Selassie Balcony, marking where the Emperor came to watch newsreels (picturehouse.com).*
>
> *Royal Victoria Park, Queen's Parade, BA1 2NJ, was opened by Princess Victoria in 1830, when she was eleven. It has fifty-seven acres of greenery and attractions, including the restored aerial walkway above its Great Dell. The lions at the Victoria Gate are copies of the Medici Lions, once of Rome, now at the Loggia dei Lanzi in Florence. It is said that Victoria never returned to the city after learning that a*

ungallant Bathonian had commented on the thickness of her ankles. But this is but one of a number of places that the Queen is supposed never to have returned to after taking offence; my favourite is Leeds, where, apparently, she was not amused when after luncheon at a hotel she was presented, in true Yorkshire fashion, with the bill.

Read:

Imperial Exile, *by Keith Bowers, 2016.*

The Coronation of Haile Selassie, *by Evelyn Waugh, 1931.*

The Emperor, by Ryszard Kapuscinski, *2006.*

Chapman-Andrews and the Emperor, *by Sir Peter Leslie, 2005*

April 1942

'ALL IN ALL, I THINK THINGS ARE GOING QUITE well. All considering. I'm forty-three now and I suppose I should face the fact that I'm never going to be famous, exactly. I've had chances, but you know how it is. I enjoyed playing when I was a boy, had lessons, but I never had any ambitions to be a classical pianist, Albert Hall, that sort of thing: Rachmaninoff, I'm not. But today's music, popular music, that's different. I've always loved that. Especially the American stuff. Berlin, Gershwin, Kern, Porter, I love playing them. I like a bit of swing, Ellington and Goodman, but I prefer the more wistful songs. Perhaps it's the times, perhaps it's because I'm Jewish, probably it's all of it. British songs tend to be a touch too treacly for me, although, obviously, I have to play them. Coward's funny stuff is good, but the sentimental ones, who needs such schmaltz? 'A Nightingale Sang In Berkeley Square,' I get a lot of requests for that, it's a cut above. I wish I'd written about angels dining at the Ritz. Here in Bath we have angels, climbing up the outside of the Abbey, but I couldn't see them at the Ritz, not posh enough. I'm getting a bit fed up with playing "We'll Meet Again", but I know why they want it. Music's important at times like these. You play a song and you can see he or she is remembering someone who isn't there. Especially when they're dining on their own. There's quite a few in this hotel on their own. Not all elderly, but mostly. That's Bath, though, isn't it? Certainly this hotel. Not big enough for a ballroom, you see, but they do like some music over dinner, keeps the silence out.

'Funny, talking about the Albert Hall when this is the Albert Hotel, or Royal Albert Hotel to give it its full moniker. Life in all its twists, eh? I play every night and then move into the lounge after dinner. I've got an upright in the restaurant, I much prefer the baby grand in the lounge. Sometimes someone will send me a drink, and there's the occasional tip, but not like the waiting staff get. They're friendly enough, but I'm a bit apart, I think they see me as different, a little exotic. Walter, the head waiter, is friendly enough, though. Been here for years, and looks like it. Every evening I come in and every evening he says the same thing, in his Bath accent, "Evenin', Maestro. Ready to tickle the ivories?"

'I also give lessons, mostly in the afternoons and weekends, interested kids, not-so-interested kids, talented, not-so-talented. I teach them at home. I've got a small house in Larkhall, it's all I need. It's just me since my mother died, five years ago. My dad went a long time ago, when I was fifteen. We moved down to Bath from Hackney. He was a watch repairer, bit of a romantic, always fancied Bath for its Regency reputation, got a job in one of the big jewellers on Milsom Street. Never really got the chance to find out if he liked it, though, killed at Ypres.

'His father was from Lubeck, came over last century. I had cousins in the German army last time. Not this time. Lost touch with the family over there, but obviously I know all about the way the Nazis have been treating the Jews, from way back in the thirties, and now it's getting worse and worse. I don't want to believe some of the stuff recently, about mass killings, just for being a Jew. Of course you ask yourself why we get treated like this, have for so long. I know all the Christ murderers stuff, but it doesn't really explain it all, does it? My dad used to say, "It's always been the same. When things go wrong, what do they do: blame the Jew," But what can we do? What can I do? Take it, as usual, I suppose, like I take the petty stuff, the snobs and the ones who think they're funny, talking about how mean we are, keen on the money. Sneer at us, but they don't mind, don't really know they're singing the songs we write and watching the films we make. There's talk about a return to Palestine, but how's that ever going to work?

'I've never married, not sure why, really, suppose the piano got in the way. And my mother. Not a typical Jewish mother, but typical enough. I've been lucky, though – too young to fight last time, too old this. Never cracked the music business properly, all the same. I've written lots of songs, I've got a bit of a gift. You may have heard some of them: "Your Eyes Have It", "Dreamy Days Down Home", "You're Dandy, I'm Handy". No? Well, like I say, I'm still waiting for the big success. I've just sent "The Dusk",

"The View and You" round the publishers. No takers. Just now, I'm working on "She Laughed in Bath"; might be able to work in some saucy lyrics. I write the music and the words, I'm a bit like Irving and Cole that way.

'I sing a bit, my voice is OK, but a threat to Mr Bing Crosby, no. Another reason why I'm in a hotel. They don't like me to sing during dinner, but I do try a few in the lounge, if the mood's right. The manager, Mr Brooks, ex-army, first show, trusts me, which is good. I can only remember one disagreement, that was over, "Yes, We Have No Bananas", which he thought was a bit "raucous" and I can see his point, I suppose.

'I usually finish around eleven o'clock. This is Bath, after all. Then I go into the kitchen and have a drink and a meal from what's left before I go. The chef, Alois, is a bit of a mensch, always ready for a chat, he likes to relax over a brandy after a hard night with the soup, chops and sponge. Funny thing is that he's from Cologne. Everyone here thinks he's French, but he had to go before an internment tribunal when the war broke out. He was given the all-clear, but as he says, "Just think how many I could kill with my cooking!" Mad thing, this war. We hear the bombers on their way to Bristol, it's getting a terrible pasting. But, as I say, this is Bath. The Admiralty have got people here, staying in all the hotels, the Empire's full of them. There's a rather nice chap staying in this hotel, as it happens. Says he was in the last show, doesn't recommend being at Jutland, keeps requesting "We'll Gather Lilacs", which can put a bit of a damper on dinner, believe me, so I play it a little quicker than Ivor Novello's dirge of a pace, who's to notice? Except of course

Lady Higginson, who's very on the ball with the music. She used to be on the halls before she married his late Lordship. She was Miss Ethel Snow, "The Dalston Songbird", but that was all a long time ago, although you can still tell she was a London girl of no great pedigree. She's fun, but failing a bit. Some of the other nobs here look down on her, but she doesn't care, so why should I?

'There are the bombers again. Funny how you hope they'll go and drop their load on some other poor schmucks. It's hardly "We're all in this together", is it? Quite a few people in Larkhall, ordinary people like me, have a bit of a josh: "You off to watch the rich people eat as much as they like at your hotel, Sammy?" It's the rationing, but that's not all of it. They say it will all change after the war. We should be so lucky. Not going very well so far, is it? But the Americans are in now, that's changing things. It went quite well tonight. I tried out "There'll Be Bluebirds Over the White Cliffs of Dover", a standard if I ever I heard one. Written by Americans, funnily enough. "We don't have bluebirds in England," said Mrs Bateman, silly old bat. Those bombers are very close, though, aren't they?'

*

'I'M NOT REALLY SURE WHY I'M IN BATH, MY DARLING. I wasn't sure what I was going to do when Francis died. We didn't have any children and I didn't want the big house in Highgate even if I could have afforded to keep it going. We didn't have a fortune, judges aren't paid that much. Not as much as I used to get, anyway, in the old days. I expect they've told you, they always do – I used to be Ethel Snow, "The Dalston Songbird". I was a star, my darling, I really was. All the old songs. "The Boy I Love is Up in the Gallery, If You Were the Only Boy in the World", all of them. Not a great voice, nothing operatic or fancy like that, but I had a gift. When I sang everyone listening thought I was singing just to them. I can't explain it any better. Vera Lynn's got it, not many more. Francis thought I was singing just to him, but then he would, he was a pompous bugger, Francis. But I made him unpompous, if that's a word. And when he wasn't being pompous, he was a sweet man with laughing eyes, although tell that to the defendant. We brought out the best in each other, apart from children, of course. I would have liked children, they're like an investment in the future, aren't they? Although what future we've got, I don't know. My future? Well, it's all right, living in a hotel, and Bath's more manageable than dear old London. I don't like cooking, either, never got the hang of it, never had to, somehow, went straight from my dear old mum's stuff to the Savoy Grill, duckie. Or something like that. Food's all right here, good chef, Alois, pretends he's French when we all know he's really a German. Must be funny for him, hearing those planes overhead. On the way to Bristol again, I suppose.

'Sam played a new Vera Lynn song tonight, in the lounge. I like Sammy, he's a good pianist, but his voice isn't really there. He's played me some of the stuff he's written, and that's better but not quite there, either. I think he'll probably be a hotel pianist for the rest of his life. I've sung with him a few times, but my voice is gone, really, and I don't want to give the jealous stuck-up bitches in this hotel the satisfaction. Especially that Mrs Bateman. She cracks herself up to be really grand, but we all know about her, too. She was married to a Lino manufacturer up north, made all his money from paying his workers as little as he could and from other poor lambs who couldn't afford anything better than his cheap floor coverings. He ran off with his secretary, that's why the old pooter's down here in this hotel. Mean bastard wouldn't pay for anything more and she couldn't stand the scandal any more than he could if she divorced him. I could get cross with her, but I feel sorry for the poor cow, really. That's always been my trouble, too soft. That's why me and Francis were such a good team, he looked after me that way. I still miss the silly old sod, even the looks over his spectacles and the way he raised his finger before saying anything, even to ask me to pass the butter. He loved me, too. I'll try and get some sleep now. Good night, Francis.'

*

'IT'S A JOB, ISN'T IT? I HAD THE BIG CAREER ON THE go before the war, when I was in London, before I was coming down here. Sous-chef at the Connaught, I was learning a lot there, and not just about the cooking. The English are all right as long as you're the polite one. You can tell them anything, that they're ugly, awkward, wrong, anything, as long as you say it the proper way, in the polite way. I didn't so I get the sack. The stupid woman shouldn't have complained about the broccoli. Undercooked! Why do they like their vegetables like the soup? I shouldn't have left the kitchen and told the ugly *frau* where she should be putting the broccoli, though. The drink didn't help. I didn't know she was the minor person of royalty. Perhaps I should, perhaps I should have noticed that the chin was as weak as she liked her broccoli. Anyway, like I says, I come down here, suits me better, less of what the English call "airs and graces", apart from that Bateman *frau*, and we know about her. They all think I'm French, but I'm actually German, which makes things a little strange. Just like the English not to know the difference! The tribunal decided I was not a threat, although I always say to Sam the pianist that I could poison a lot of people. Not sure it would matter much here, they're all so old. Widows and a few old soldiers fighting the last war, grumbling they would never have had to get out at Dunkirk.

'I suppose I can't help having the feeling to be a little proud of the Germans, even though I've been here longer than I was ever there. I wouldn't be fighting for them, but some of my family are fighting, I think, we're not really in touch, for the obvious reasons. There's bad stories coming out of there, but who do you believe? Sam's a Jew, but he doesn't make much of it. I've never had any quarrel with them, but there are the stories about them, too, aren't there? We don't get Jews in this hotel, lots of the English don't like them, especially the posh English, or the ones who think they are posh. I'm talking with Sam, but we're not talking about that. There are the bombers, must be on the way to Bristol, pity the poor people there. Bombed by my people. I think I'll think about tomorrow's menu. Here comes Sammy now.'

*

'GINNY AND ME OFTEN COME TO THE ASSEMBLY Rooms on a Saturday night, for the dance, and it would take more than Adolf to stop us. Yes, we like the idea that dances have been going on here since the days of Beau Nash and all the smart people. We get quite dressed up, best suit and frock and that, but nothing like then, I imagine, with the crinolines and everything. The music's a bit different, too, isn't it? No minuets now! Charleston, foxtrot, quickstep, that sort of thing. I'm rather proud of my Chassé Reverse Turn, there's posh. We met here, as it happens. I saw Ginny across a crowded floor, and although it wasn't exactly love at first sight, we often say we knew. Funny thing, Ginny stood on my foot rather than the other way round, we did laugh. They say Bath's not what it was, but we like it, I think all that roistering would have been a bit rich for us! You sometimes get a sense of the old place, not here, too noisy, but sometimes in the streets of a night, on the short cut home, a shadow, a flutter, a laugh, I fancy even sometimes a "Gad, Sir!" Happened again only the other week, near the Royal Albert, that's on our way home. Ginny thinks it's the beer, but I've got my links: I'm supposed to be related to the Tom Atkins who had the first Bath Oliver shop.

That's why I'm called Tom. Bit of a shame there's been no money out of it, though. Ginny and I run a newsagents up on Bear Flat. Better be getting back, I suppose. There's some RAF chaps over there, very lively, but with a lot about them, makes you feel safe to know they're on our side. Be glad when it's all over and our boy Jack's back. Haven't seen him for eighteen months now, but he writes, doesn't tell us much though. Makes you feel a bit guilty, him out there, us safe at home. Lot of grumbling in the shop about the war, but I don't see what choice we had, more it goes on, more you hear about what the Jerries are up to. My dad was always going on about them, he was in the first lot. Come on, Ginny, let's go.'

*

'I'VE BEEN DOWN HERE FOR A FEW MONTHS NOW. Admiralty, hush-hush, shorten the war by at least twelve months, they say. They say. I've listened to "them" too often in my time. "They" said we'd breeze Jutland. Not how it turned out. Wouldn't recommend that to anybody. Grey day, fear in the gut, waiting for the one that's got your tub on it. Give me sudden and instant annihilation, not that. Anyway, things not going at all well, if you ask me. Better not, I'm not marvellous for morale. Too old, seen too much. Morale's a tricky thing, disappears just like that. Fine, the Americans coming in, but we need a big victory. Soon. Dunkirk, Battle of Britain, excellent, but no sense of a turned tide, just a check, and now waiting for the next thing. Fine for morale, did I say? I've just realised I've been requesting "We'll Gather Lilacs in the Spring Again" every night since Thursday. Must be the claret. Very good pianist here, though, talented chap, played it again earlier. We've had a few chats. Jewish, of course, and all that. Better turn in before the ghastly Mrs Bateman grabs me. Probably feel brighter in the morning.'

*

'RIPPINGMOST FUN, STAYING IN A HOTEL. I'M JUST visiting from school, Ma and Pa sent me away, up north and out of it. Bit over the top if you ask me, and, by the cringe, you should taste the grub, pigswill, dishwater. Rugger's v good, though, and the chaps are fine. Wizard stodge here, a real French chef, says the Pater. He says it's safer here than at home. Safety, safety: we'd all like a bit of fuss, much better than maths, thank you. Pa's just visiting, too. He looks quite strange, different, in his uniform. Apart from that, he doesn't seem to have changed much, I still call him "Sir". Not like Ma. She's pale and snippy and keeps hugging me, which is pretty embarrassing, actually. My sister Dolly is with us, she's six and a bit tiresome. I like Bath. We visited the Roman baths yesterday. I put my hand in the water and pretended to throw Dolly in, Ma got really cross, and made a big stink about it. I wish I could cheer her up a bit. I tried a couple of the latest jokes, but they didn't work, sample, "Why did the lobster blush? Because it saw the Queen Mary's bottom." Everybody loves that at school. Even Pa smiled, but Ma just said it was rude. We're having lunch at the Grand Pump Room Hotel tomorrow, then it's my birthday next week, I've asked for a toy Spitfire and more soldiers. I'm going to sleep now, oh do put a sock in it and stop gassing, Dolly.'

*

'I DIDN'T SET OUT TO BE A HOTEL MANAGER. REGULAR, infantry regiment, second lieutenant when the last show broke out. Thought I'd make a career out of it, but France changed all that. Trenches, mud, rats, filth, waiting, shelling, waiting, tedious comrades, annoying comrades, frightened comrades, screaming comrades, the noise, the death. I was all right to begin with, but each time we went up I got worse, and each time we went back I found it harder and harder not to think about going back up again. Some sort of terrible joke of a game, the spin of roulette, musical trenches, would you be in the front line when the order came to go over the top or safe out of it behind? Five days every thirty, six to one, not good odds, but not bad enough to get resigned to, almost a relief when you heard there was to be an attack, but that didn't last long. Can't remember how many times I went over the top because I don't want to, don't want to remember the deaths, the sheer bloody chaos, the pointless raids, the terror, waiting in the shellholes on a raid, listening to them, the enemy, poor bastards like us. Don't want to think about why I was one of the survivors, I've always hated the strain of having to make something of myself because they couldn't. I got injured a couple of times, shrapnel in the leg, lost a finger, this one, hoped it would be worse, certainly enjoyed the morphine, not the coming to, not the going back to that smell of shit and piss and corpses and the screams in the silence and the night. I ended up a lieutenant with nightmares and a tremor. I couldn't face staying in, wasn't really qualified for anything else. Father knew old Barnes, the owner here, came for a meal here, took me on. I own the place to all intents and purposes now, look after it for Barnes's widow, Nelly, a good sort. There's not much difference between leading a platoon and running a hotel. The flies in the ointment, the disrupters of discipline, the untrained, are of course the guests. I find the best way is to treat them like an immediately superior officer, just deferential enough and giving nothing away. And I befriend no one, guest or staff, it only leads to trouble. I quite like Sam the pianist, Jewish but no harm in that, I knew Sassoon in the war, mad as a snake, Baghdadi family, attractive but too mad for me. I loved Lennie, how I loved Lennie, but they killed him at Cambrai. Not a day, Lennie, I don't think about your touch on my cheek in that shabby little place in Armentieres, your eyes locked with mine, close as our embrace, loving looks, loving arms, the feel of your body, the delicious man smell of you. Not a day. Never been interested in anyone else, probably haven't allowed it. A few fumblings early on, but too risky. And now war again. Sassoon lives not far away, but I've never tried to look him up. Saw him in Bath, once, but I didn't approach him. He keeps himself to himself, thinks he should have died with Owen, which in a way he did, like me with Lennie. Listen, Germans above, got to control the shakes, and the ghosts, still waiting for the bang and oblivion.'

*

'COMMANDER LEES HAS TAKEN A BIT OF A SHINE to me, I think. Not that surprising, I've kept my figure, neat bust, nothing vulgar, thank you, and my cheekbones help, one of my best features, I've always thought, along with my excellent posture, of course. I pride myself on my conversation as well. I'm quite the authority on Bath now, Regency and Roman, able to keep a conversation going very well, I like history, it's about my sort of people. I don't advertise my knowledge, of course, but I did feel I had to correct the commander when he talked about the pineapples on the pediments in the Circus. Acorns, I said, acorns, the architect, Mr Wood, was very keen on them. It was because of his name, Wood, trees, do you see. I like Jane Austen, too, but I don't agree with the people who think she's funny. Sir Walter Elliot is a particular favourite of mine, very proper insistence on the order of things.

'Very different from my Walter, or should I say was-my-Walter. He had absolutely no sense of the right way to behave. Not so surprising when he came up from nothing, but I've managed it very well if I do say it myself. No one in Bath would suspect that Mrs Bateman was born in Leach Street with a common accent. You do have to work at it, though. All those elocution lessons with Miss Welsby on Croppers Hill, I've how-nowed enough cows for a lifetime, I have. Not like Lady Higginson. On the halls and proud of it, for some reason. Oh, they make a fuss of her here, but she doesn't impress me. Once a floozy. Like the one stupid Walter took up with. "We love each other, Hattie," he said, and how silly did that sound from a man with a Lino factory? He just couldn't see what she was after wasn't his little pot belly but his brass, silly old beggar. I expect Lady Higginson's sainted husband wasn't much of an oil painting, either. But there's all sorts of goings-on going on during this war, not like the last one, when people still knew how to behave, when we were all behind our lads, not grumbling and muttering like now. I was only a girl, but that's how I remember it. They say this war is going to change things, but I don't see why it should, what's wrong with the way things have been? And if change means everyone's going to be the same, floozies and respectable, spivs and honest people, the great unwashed and people who've worked very hard to better themselves, I rather not be part of that, I don't want to see it, thank you very much. People really are the giddy limit, aren't they? I wonder if Commander Lees is married.'

*

'NOT LONG TO MY PENSION NOW. I'VE EARNED IT, over fifty years of being polite to some terrible people. Well, that's a bit unfair, I suppose, that's a grumpy old head waiter talking. There have been a fair few who've been pleasant enough. The test isn't whether they give you a tip, but whether they bother to find out your name, and then remember it. Things have been loosening up ever since the last show, went quiet after it, and then completely diddlecome and barmy in the twenties, remember? Me, I've just got on with it and everybody, that's the way. Let the waiters know you know more than them, mind, and let the manager know he knows more than you even though he doesn't. Mr Brooks, he's been here a few years, nice chap, but very reserved. Not stuck-up, reserved, lot of ex-trench officers like that, no point trying to get close. Bad nerves. But he lets me get on with it. I think he's got more of an eye on Alois, for obvious reasons, something to do with him being a German, others to do with him being a bit bolshy. Chefs, though, never met one who wasn't a bit diddlecome, either. Diddlecome? Old Somerset word for crazy. I'm a Bath boy, love Bath. Some people live in a place and take it for granted, but not me. Bath is where I'm to. I love the stories of the old days, and walking through the old places. The sights you see! We've had the Emperor of Abyssinia, old Haile Selassie himself, staying here these past few years after the Eyeties chucked him out. I often used to see him walking about at night with his giant servant and his little dogs. This lot here used to say I was making it up, but I've seen him all right. And I don't drink. You ask Elsie. Well, you could have asked Elsie, she's been gone a few years now, I'm on my own. They say the Emperor's gone off to get his country back, good luck to him, he was well liked here. There's other people to see as well, if you have the eyes. Sometimes I see Lord Nelson. He was smiling last time, so I reckon we're going to be all right. I wonder who I'll see tonight.'

*

'I've been to Bath before. It was a few years ago now, in the thirties. A bit shabby, I thought, living on its past, without the style. But nothing could take away that gasp when you round the corner and see the Royal Crescent for the first time. What panache that man John Wood had! I've knocked around Europe a fair amount, and I know that trick of the old cathedral builders, the winding concealed approach through narrow streets then – bang! – there it is. Compostella has the best, I think, but I don't know of any secular building that pulls it off as well as the Crescent. But then there is something religious about Wood, isn't there? The bare ethereal elegance of the Crescent moving into the dense decoration of the Circus, the moon and the sun, the old religion, these two temples set in a valley, surrounded by wood and forest. The Enlightenment was partly and particularly pagan, and the Georgians in Bath were among its finest mature exponents, until the inevitable reaction and the Victorians, and Bath was never the same again. Listen to me, though, clearly getting nostalgic for the old days. Not an academic anymore, no. No call for it, not until all this is sorted out, at least, one way of the other. We should come to Bath any moment now. And if we survive Bath, York and Canterbury are also promised.

'So, an irony, but by no means the greatest, in such times, a young lecturer in European history about to bomb one of its finest adornments. Oh, I know the arguments, they did it to us at Lubeck and Rostock, set out to level our precious fine medieval masterpieces, just to show us they can. We've heard about the bells of St Mary's at Lubeck, crashed 400 feet to the floor. British lecturers in European history are no doubt also getting excellent views through their sights. But surely it's not only the historians who can see this has always been the way, blood and money and more and more people shedding blood over money and land and power, egged on, led by deranged personalities. Any historian knows that all Europe's great leaders and most of the mediocre ones have been certifiable. Is the present one worse than Napoleon, madder than Joan of Arc or the Spanish Philip or the Kaiser? Perhaps it is only historians who remember the horror of the Thirty Years' War, twelve million dead.

'And I am a historian, I know how it starts. If things have been very bad and are now getting better, do you worry that you're being led by a madman and his madmen? If things are getting better, do you worry about those for whom they are not? Do you not turn away from such inconveniences? Treat the truth as a lie? The mad make us mad. Why else am I up here, about to obliterate beauty? I don't want to think about what I will not be able to see, the people down there. I don't want to think about the terrible futility, about the madness of trying to conquer and control the world. The Romans, even here, the British and their empire, everywhere, and now this, the maddest until the madder comes along. The historian finally realises that knowledge is nothing to the madness, the invincible power of the madness. And now I have to do my mad work, because I am weak as well as mad, and pray to a god who mustn't exist that he will preserve this Dornier. And Bath.'

Afterword

BATH WAS BOMBED IN THREE RAIDS ON TWO successive nights in April, 1942: over 400 people were killed and another 1,000 injured; The raids were declared to be in retaliation for RAF attacks on Lubeck, in which some 300 people were killed and nearly 800 injured; and Rostock, in which over 200 people were killed and nearly 100 injured. There are arguments about the amounts of responsibility borne by the two sides for deliberately targeting cities and their peoples, but not about the hideous toll of lives, injuries and general and particular destruction in Europe between 1939 and 1945.

The novel, ironic, and more than a little deranged feature of these raids, which followed a lull after the London Blitz ended in May, 1941, was the intent to destroy the finest examples of the two countries' historic and civilised achievements. The bombing of Bath formed part of the so-called Baedeker Blitz, named for the famous German cultural guidebook; the Luftwaffe also attacked York, Norwich, Exeter and Canterbury, killing over

1,600 people and destroying priceless pieces of antiquity. Coventry Cathedral and the city's medieval centre were destroyed in 1940. You might find the comparison with Isis and Palmyra instructive.

In Bath, the bombing destroyed over 200 buildings of historical importance, including the former homes of Jane Austen, De Quincey, and RICHARD BRINSLEY SHERIDAN (1751–1816), Irishman, wit, playwright, parliamentarian, eloper from Bath with the beautiful singer Elizabeth Linley, duellist for her honour, and creator of Mrs Malaprop, the word-mangling wonder of his famed play set in the city, The Rivals, as with: 'She is as headstrong as an allegory on the banks of the Nile.'

Lansdown, Holloway, Oldfield Park, Bear Flat and Twerton were especially affected. The west wing of Dr Oliver's hospital was also severely damaged. But it could have been worse. The Abbey and the Roman baths were not hit. The Royal Crescent, the Circus, Queen's Square, the Assembly Rooms and the Paragon were hit but not devastated; all have been restored, as has Dr Oliver's lost wing.

The Francis Hotel, along the south side of Queen's Square, lost its frontage, but casualties were thankfully light, as most of the guests and staff had taken shelter in the basement. Guests and staff at the Regina Hotel in Bennett Street did not fare so well. The hotel had similarly reinforced its basement, but not everyone got there when the sirens sounded around midnight: twenty-seven people died and half the hotel was destroyed in a direct hit. The Royal Albert Hotel is based on the Regina Hotel, but the characters bear no resemblance to the reality. There were three raids on Bath in quick succession. The fictional events at the Royal Albert take place before the first bombing at around 11pm on Saturday, April 25. The attackers returned at around 4am on Sunday, April 26. The bomb that fell on the Regina came in the third attack, in the earliest hour of Monday, April 27.

The city's air defences were inadequate. It was protected by the RAF flying from Charmy Down and Colerne; Squadron Leader Denis 'Splinters' Smallwood, twenty-four, was in a group that had to scramble back to Charmy Down from the dance at the Assembly Rooms on the Saturday. Night fighting was an infant art: 'We painted the aircraft black and relied on our eyeballs and that's about all the technology we had,' Air Chief Marshal Smallwood recalled many years later. Only four German bombers were shot down, with a further five probables destroyed by anti-aircraft fire on their way back to France. Three of the planes downed over Bath were Dorniers. There were no further raids.

The broken and plummeted bells of St Mary's in Lubeck still rest where they fell, not far from where the church's famous Dance of Death was also burnt and destroyed in the raid. Near the bells is an inscription in English: 'For peace and reconciliation. The Cathedral of Coventry was destroyed on 10 November 1940 by German aviators. Allied bombers set fire to St Mary's on Palmarum [Palm Sunday] 1942 (28th to 29th March). The bells plummeted from the burning south tower into the depths of the chapel. Two bells are here bursting as a reminder against war and violence.' On the chapel wall close by hangs the Cross of Coventry, made from the wreckage of that cathedral, a gift of reconciliation from its congregation.

The larger bell dates from 1689. Its inscription, perhaps even more powerful, translates as: 'To preach, to prayer. I also ring to the corpses. I mean War. I mean Fire. I also give signs of joy and peace. Jesus grant that in peace and joy I always sound. Turn away from this city plague, fire, raid.'

Amen to that.

See:

The Bath War Memorial is situated in Queen's Parade, at the main entrance to Royal Victoria Park, BA1 2NJ. It commemorates the 2,194 people of Bath killed by war, at home and abroad, since 1914.

Read:

Bath Blitz, *by Martin Wainwright, 1981.*
Bath Blitz Memorial Project *(bathblitz.org).*

Near Angels

It had been her idea to come to Bath. He had wanted to meet nearer her home, as she would be more comfortable, more relaxed, more amenable. Perhaps a local wine bar, he had suggested, that would be the ticket. But she preferred somewhere between them. Bath would be nice. Did he know it?

He did know Bath and didn't much care for it. Everyone always seemed faintly conscious they were in Bath, on a set, to be seen. But the Georgians had taken all the rackety fun with them, and now it was just old, like most of the inhabitants. Not that he wasn't getting on himself, and rackety. His name spoke loudly of it. Clive was a believer in nominative determinism; he felt that what he was called had removed some element of choice in his progress through life, had somehow made inevitable the travelling with the samples, the coupons, the dabbling in estate agency, financial advice and fancy bathrooms – just sign here, please – and all the other innovative selling schemes, the blazers and the golf clubs where he fancied he had cut something of a dash. This was the way of the Clive. Small wonder Clive Lewis had preferred to be known as CS. And where were all the Clives now?

A seagull keened harshly and considered him without enthusiasm. They were all over Bath, brought in by the rich rubbish tip pickings, but they offended Clive's sense of place: he liked his seagulls by the sea, if at all. Actually, that would be a good name for a pub: The Incongruous Gull. Clive spent a lot of time thinking inconsequentially like this. He blamed it for his lack of success, his tendency to stray. He shifted on his bench in the square or circus or whatever it was and rubbed where his moustache had been. He had an hour before meeting June. He'd cocked the train times up, numbers were not really his thing, bit rum for a financial adviser, obviously, but there you are, and he hadn't wanted to be late. Quite a sharp breeze was blowing in from the Bristol Channel, even for November, but he didn't want to go to the cafe just yet, he financially advised himself.

June, though. A good name: a June had no airs and graces, like with a, say, Sophie, or a Caroline, but did have that bit of a twinkle lacked by a, say, Sarah, or a Susan. True, June's photograph on the Lovemedo website hadn't disclosed much of this anticipated *joie de vivre*, nor her emails; and it was also true that Clive's wife had been called Constance and she'd left him. Still, Clive felt June had warmed a little to his *bon mots* and generous use of exclamation marks. And she had agreed to meet him.

Since losing Constance, there had been a succession of girls, as he was still accustomed to call them, even though none of them would see fifty again, nor, as it invariably turned out, him. Sometimes, when he was facing the future without his usual forced jauntiness, he wondered if online dating services might ever be able to come up with a life partner who would entrust her savings to a recently discharged bankrupt presently if intermittently telephoning strangers in usually vain attempts to persuade them to buy recycled solar panels at a special one-off price in advance while his excellent firm was in the area.

But there is something about Clive, despite the scuffed suede shoes, and the novelty banana cufflinks that change colour from green to yellow depending on temperature (never really caught on, for some reason). He is not a bad man, more a not very good one. He has made his mistakes, but, generally, he has been punished for them, as Constance would agree, if she could be found. Clive's money would be on Brighton, or Benidorm, or Margate, depending on how much is left of Clive's money, or rather the money unwisely placed by the unwise with Clive as part of his Easter Bunny Chocolate Egg Club, Royal Pets Through the Centuries mugs, From Bowler to Burqa: Celebrating Diverse Britain figurines, the Great Liberal Democrat Leaders set of souvenir plates, and all the rest of his imaginative but ultimately disappointing enterprises. Clive will tell you that the shortcomings of such ventures were sadly but entirely the fault of overseas suppliers, the recession, and unsympathetic and appallingly run banks punishing enterprise while at the same time paying out excessive bonuses to undeserving employees. And you will find yourself disposed to believe what Clive tells you, because Clive has convinced himself it is true, and will become quite hot under his well-worn collar about it. In more reflective mood, Clive will allow that over-enthusiasm and impetuousness might have played a small part; that and sheer bad luck. After a few more, he might also turn to thoughts of Constance, muse bitter-sweetly at her blonde memory and the cruel, inexplicable abandonment. Right now, though, Clive was thinking it was a shame he hadn't been able to persuade June to meet him in one of Bath's quite reasonably priced restaurants, Amandini's or somewhere like that, where he could have used his 'oh my goodness where's my wallet' routine. The November dusk was drawing in; the wind had dropped, but it was still cold, the sort of day to make a man feel old and think of the thick fogs and warm fires of his youth. Clive got up, aimed a sketchy suede kick at the incongruous gull and began to make his way to the cafe.

*

CONSTANCE RATHER LIKED THE VICTORIA ART GALLERY, municipal Bath's major visual arts offering. Some preferred the zappier, zeitgeistier and altogether more happening Holburne, over Pulteney Bridge and up by Sydney Gardens, but June found the Victoria's collection, with its Gainsboroughs and Lawrences, comforting. Even the Turner was a comparatively bland early watercolour of the Master's. But if she wanted something more exciting there was always the prodigy Barker's *Bride of Death*, pale, wan, abed and breathing her last the night before the wedding. Constance tended to follow that by going over to Herbert Henry La Thangue's merry gaggle of geese charging out of the big picture towards her, which usually cheered her up.

She had come late to art, and was still a little defensive towards the abstract, although some progress had been made lately with Kandinsky and Heron, and even Mondrian. In fact, Constance had come late to most of her senses. The seventies hadn't quite been the sixties, but she'd certainly had what they used to call a blast, involving, so far as she remembered, boutique-assisting, chalet-girling, some light hospitality and PR work, one marriage and several other failed relationships that had seemed fun at the time. By the end of the nineties, though, she was coming to realise that there wasn't a great deal available for a blonde beginning to fade to grey generally and specifically and resorting to various bottles for both colour and cheer. A dispiriting round of demonstrating kitchen appliances and promoting packet sauces led her to the Craft and Hobby Fair at Harrogate, where she found herself on the Painting by Numbers ('*Now you too can be Van Gogh!*') stand next to the Motorway Service Stations of Great Britain part-work stand, manned by Clive. A little older than Constance, he made her laugh and forget the dreary dwindle of the days, with his bad jokes and fine line in anecdote ('*So bang went another fortune!*'). He rather reminded her of her father, before he left. An affair grew into an arrangement and soon and somehow they were a married couple, living in Cheltenham for some reason she had now forgotten (good for the motorway?), their time mostly spent travelling to and standing at craft and hobby fairs, part of that restless group, successors to the old commercial travellers, who tell themselves that flogging themselves and their costume jewellery, or health tonics, or pashminas, or pet baskets, or Motorway Services Stations of Great Britain part-works will suddenly result in it all 'taking off' and making them rich beyond avarice, and, until it happens, you really can't beat working for yourself, even if all the unloading and frantic reloading of your Volvo afterwards does threaten to break your back and your spirit at times. So they continue to bear the irritating indifference of the punters ('*Not today, thank you*') and the irritating repetitious bravado of their fellow traders ('*Yes, a pretty good day, all in all!*') who have similarly not yet 'taken off', and never will.

Looking back, Constance couldn't quite understand how Clive had persuaded her to persevere with all this. Not all optimism is catching. But there seemed to be enough money, with the fairs supplemented by the subscriptions coming in for Clive's various enterprises, the collectable series of plates and figurines, the small savings clubs designed to finance treats, like the Easter Chocolate Bunny Club. Looking back, Constance couldn't quite understand how she'd failed to spot that the money should have been spent on Chinese factories churning out plates, figurines, chocolate bunnies, and part-works, and not on Clive and Constance. Eventually, over the very reasonable eat-all-you-can Sunday buffet at one of those expense-spared approximations of a gastro pub just outside Godalming, Clive mentioned that 'things' were getting 'a bit tight'. He was being pursued by numbers of disappointed subscribers and the bank was being completely bloody unreasonable. 'We'll get through somehow, Connie, worry not,' he had said, taking another sip of the under-curated guest beer and raising his glass to the detached landlady, who didn't notice. Constance knew they wouldn't get through somehow; the bad news, in a place like that, so far from past chic and hopes for more, laid a cold hand on her heart. She saw nothing but trouble ahead. Still, at least he was a gent, Clive, and a bit of an old romantic: how much in love do you have to be to want a joint bank account? On the Monday, Constance transferred the little that was left; and left, too. For richer, for poorer, in sickness and in health; but, please, God, no, not for cheap buffeting every Sunday at the Fox and Hounds or other holes in corners of unambitious complacency. With a quick frown at the memory, Constance left the Victoria, paused to do up her coat and made her way past Bath Abbey in the November dusk, smiling at the famous angels, set in stone, eternally struggling up and down ladders between heaven and earth. Why didn't they fly?

*

CLIVE TOYED WITH HIS BUN. THERE WAS ONLY SO MUCH pre-eating you could reasonably persuade somebody else to pay for, in his experience. Besides, his first bite had met a currant harder than *University Challenge*, and he really couldn't afford, in any sense, to lose another tooth, crown, or even, he sadly allowed to himself, a filling. This was the sort of minor, but nagging, discomfort that lack of money brought to a middle-class kind of life, however rackety. A new blazer and decent haircut wouldn't go amiss, either. Then he smiled, carefully concealing the temporary and increasingly loose crown that had been on Six Top Right for seven months and for which he still owed the disturbingly young dentist £200. He had remembered one of his favourite jokes: 'Did you hear about the man who drowned in a bowl of muesli? He was pulled down by a strong currant.' Clive loved the image of a man being pulled down by a strong currant. He took another sip of tea. In one more minute, June would be late. Sometimes they didn't come at all; Clive was also quite good at spotting the ones who took a quick glance from outside and then disappeared. Nothing so far; he'd give it another ten minutes. He started to list famous dentists: Dr Crippen, Doc Holliday, the South African one who used to fizz down the wing for Leeds, Wilf Rosenberg, the Flying Dentist. The Flying Dentist! Marvellous. Thus, as ever, Clive when faced with crisis. At the bankruptcy hearing, he'd kept calm by naming the Tottenham Hotspur 1961 double winning team to himself. When Constance left, he'd had to go through the losing Burnley side in the Spurs 1962 Cup Final triumph as well. Adam Blacklaw, for example, fine goalkeeper, but condemned in the memory always to be sent the wrong way by Danny Blanchflower's penalty. Perhaps if they'd had children. Back on that track again, bored with it, too long ago, leave it. June was promising, let's concentrate. Current favourite television programme, *Antiques Roadshow*; former favourite, the *National Lottery Draw*; magazines, *Country Life* and *Investors Chronicle*. Clive thought, given all this, that he could probably live with her favourite author, Jane Austen, and favourite music, *The Messiah*. A European river cruise at least seemed a certainty. Clive smiled as he always did when he remembered the delightful name of one of the operators, Viking River Cruises, picturing some particularly robust passengers arriving at swiftly abandoned destinations. It wasn't entirely clear what June did for a living; 'professional' these days covered everything from judging to footballing, and seemed most popular with what used to be called 'public servants'. But no one was a servant now, although everybody seemed to be in the services sector. Clive was having one of his blazer moments. The Polish waitress was staring at him meaningfully rather than respectfully. He smiled another careful smile and took another careful sip. It was properly dark outside now. Then Constance came in.

*

'CONNIE!' HE SPLUTTERED, SPILLING THE LAST OF HIS tea into the saucer and getting to his feet clumsily, 'It's you!'

She smiled broadly at him, enjoying his surprise. 'Yes, it's me. How are you, Clive?'

'I'm all right, I'm all right. Surprised to see *you*, obviously! How are you? Sit down, sit down!'

'I'm fine. A little older, naturally, and a bit wiser, hopefully.'

She did look older, Clive thought among all the other thoughts, including that he was a bit hot, which was never a good look. She had let her hair go grey, and was wearing it short. She'd put on weight, too. But she still looked nothing like the photograph.

'Well,' he said, 'this is a bit of a facer. I wasn't expecting you, of all people. You do like your surprises, Connie, don't you?' Clive beckoned the Polish waitress over while thinking back to the last surprise she had given him, rather the reverse of this one.

Constance sat down. She was feeling surprisingly composed. Clive was looking older, less carefully groomed, a little shiny at the edges, not only of his blazer. More vulnerable, she thought, with a sympathy that also surprised her. 'Yes, well, I'm sorry about that, Clive. I wasn't then, but I am now. It was just that things seemed so hopeless and you couldn't see it, you were still full of your usual maddening certainty that everything was going to be all right, whatever. It was brave, almost heroic in its way, and in my way I rather loved you for it, but I couldn't stand the life we were living anymore, the mean, miserable falseness of it. I don't suppose you've changed.'

The Polish waitress delivered two cups of tea and a selection of cakes that were as tired as her expression. Clive patted his blazer pockets. 'You've lost your wallet,' said Constance. Clive smiled the rueful smile, the one she'd always liked. A temporary crown was in temporary touch with one of his teeth. He needed a haircut; what had been tousled was now wispy.

'Sorry, darling,' he said, 'Just reflex.'

'Like the "darling",' said Constance.

Clive looked surprised. 'That's right, that's right.' He did some more distracted patting. 'Actually, you're not going to believe this, but I really have lost my wallet.' They both laughed, and found it comfortable. 'Not that there was anything much in it', he said. 'You did rather clean me out, you know', he added, giving her his old recriminating look, the one where his head went down and he looked out mournfully from under his eyebrows. 'Where did you go? Was it Benidorm? Barbados?' He gave her his rueful smile again.

'Do me a favour, Clive. How much do you think was in the account? There was barely enough to get to Bridlington.'

'What did you do, then? Did you invest our money wisely? Or win the lottery?'

'Both, actually. I bought a Lotto ticket with it, and won £20,000. I got a job in an antiques shop. I'm pretty good at selling if you remember, especially when I'm interested, and it's not chocolate bunnies or motorway service station partworks.'

Clive winced. 'We were just unlucky there. The time wasn't quite right. We could have done it. People are fascinated by service stations. I know a man who can recite the M6 ones, both ways, and then there's Chigwell, on the the M11, which has never been built, and Happendon, great name, on the M74, you can get haggis there, you know–' He broke off, recognising Connie's smile, and finding again how much he loved it, how much he would love it to go on full beam, crinkles and dimples and bright eyes in top beguilement. 'Sorry, I was forgetting you've heard all this before. OK, the ideas were crap. Not much better since, to be honest, either. Unless you fancy some solar panels. We are in your area.'

The jokes were still there, and the brittle brightness, but this Clive was a frayed, afraid Clive. Constance's sudden, unexpected appearance had cracked the customary front, the cheerful confidence that was his security, his protection against the truth, whether about his failures, or his doubts, or the need to be loved, and not to be left, even or especially if you are nearly sixty, overweight, and pretty broke. And especially not to be left, he realised, by Connie, who had almost smiled at the solar panel sally. He'd prepared lots of carefully insouciant stuff for this meeting, if it ever happened – 'I'm sorry about Godalming, Clive'; 'Ah, yes, Godalming, I remember it well. You were in blue, the bathroom suite was avocado'. But his nursed hurt had melted away before the reality of her, and with the realisation that he had, in fact, been a silly old fool. He wanted to tell her he still loved her, would always love her, could they start again, he'd be sensible this time, wouldn't touch the Lotto money, no, couldn't think what had made him think of that. Instead, he said, 'I see there's a performance of *The Messiah* at the Abbey next week. Fancy it?'

'I'd love to,' said Constance. 'I've taken up singing in a choir. We did *The Messiah* last year. Such fantastically infinite, transcending, moving music, and so good for letting and getting everything out. It helps me relax, and sometimes I really need that. But you were never into choral singing before, Clive. Those sailors singing "There is Nothin' Like a Dame: in *South Pacific* was about as far as you went in that direction.'

'You never used words like "transcending" before. Isn't that something to do with gender? Sorry, a bit feeble, best I could manage at short notice. To be honest,

I found there was only so much consolation you could get from Rodgers and Hammerstein, and "You'll Never Walk Alone" didn't quite cut it, given the circumstances. I've missed you, Connie.'

Clive had to work hard to resist saying, 'I'd grown accustomed to your face', even though it was Lerner and Loewe and one of the worst things he could have said. He had this compulsion to lighten conversations, try jokes, especially bad ones, because it was much easier than revealing that he was hurt and afraid and lonely and frightened that she might laugh at silly old Clive.

'You have changed, Clive, haven't you? Before, you wouldn't have been able to say you missed me without rushing to add something silly like "I'd grown accustomed to your face", because you couldn't stand being honest and leaving yourself open to the slightest possibility of rejection. You always had to have your comedy escape clause.'

She'd changed, too, Clive told himself as she looked across at him with the old smile. He took refuge behind his cup and a Bourbon biscuit that was just on the turn from crunch to crumple. More confident, certainly more intelligent than he remembered; his blonde assumptions had probably got in the way, then, and his need to be in charge, not to be threatened. And he certainly wasn't the brightest doily in the tea shop himself, as life had tended to prove, a mind wasted on trivia, frightened of the bigger things, like love.

Constance busied herself in turn with the tea pot and a fig roll that could look the Bourbon biscuit right in the eye in terms of peerage. This was pretty stupid, she told herself, even if it had seemed a good idea at the time. Clive was the past, the insecure past, the charade, the brassy self-deceit, before the silence when the hubbub dies and you're left with just yourself. She was more honest with herself now, more comfortable. She'd started taking notice, opening up, the art, the antiques, the singing, the interested attendance at small arts and book festivals. She'd not long been back from an educational cruise to the Black Sea, guest lecturers and bracing excursions. Clive was at best a river cruise man, large lunches and yellow pullovers up the Rhine, the comfortable annual break from the golf club. Still, he had volunteered *The Messiah*. And he was Clive. How many people do you meet in your life that you feel easy with, really easy, effortlessly easy? In her case, Clive. And so what if the luck of that draw gives you someone less than Samson-like, someone who's feckless, frivolous, but essentially and unfashionably kind of heart? The sex hadn't been great, admittedly, but there had been a fine and cuddly quality to it, and she had never given up entirely on coaxing Clive into something more lively. He was now telling her a joke about a man being drowned in muesli and her laughter was partly at herself for getting so ahead of herself: sex! Clive was looking across at her, delighted at her laughter, his face winningly open and affectionate. She thought of the lyrics from "My Funny Valentine", Rodgers with the great Hart this time, the one which like so many others Clive played too often, with Ella Fitzgerald as usual exactly between plaintive and piquant; the one where the fallible flawed flabby hero of the title still manages to make his lover smile with her heart. Smile with her heart! Clive!

*

Connie was giving him that full crinkle of a smile. He began to doubt his luck on this cold, grey November day. 'Blimey, I've missed that laugh, Connie!' he said. What other joke could he tell her? He didn't have many new ones. Perhaps this was the moment to be brave and tell her how much he loved her and how lonely he had been without her and could they please try again. After all, she must want that, too, or she wouldn't have gone to all this trouble finding him, so how risky could it be? Clive, new Clive, took the plunge. 'Connie, would you like to–'

In the way of these things, this was the moment the Polish waitress chose to enquire, with even less than the usual sincerity, 'Is everything all right for you?'

'More tea, Connie?' Clive continued.

'Yes, please,' said Constance. 'Cake?'

Connie looked over at the slightly collapsed half of chocolate gateau in pride of place on the counter. 'No, thank you,' she said. The waitress, inscrutable, went off. They looked at each other in the silence that always follows. 'Is this a seventies tribute cafe you've chosen, Clive?' she said. 'What next, fondue?'

Clive gave one of his happy sniggers. He'd forgotten how much he liked being teased by Connie. 'This is really amazing,' he said. 'I can't believe it. I know this sounds terribly old hat, but I hadn't realised how much I missed you. I've been lonely, really lonely since you left, Connie, but it isn't just that. I've tried to find someone else, but it hasn't worked. The ones who clearly thought I was a silly, rather pathetic specimen, with the jokes and the blazer, were only marginally outnumbered by the ones who obviously thought I was principally interested in their money. True in both cases, I suppose. But you know the jokes and the blazer are just the sad armour I wear to face the world, to get by. Hark to me, though: "sad armour". I'm not much of a knight, am I? Hardly once a night, if you remember. But I'm only the real me when I'm with you, Connie, and I like the real me more than the knight me, and I want to drop all the crap and bluster, and be with you. Connie–'

With repeated impeccable timing, the waitress arrived with the tea, sans gateau. For once in his overly aware life, Clive took no notice. 'I love you, Connie, will you come back to me?'

The waitress paused, waiting. Connie looked at him with the sweetest smile, wrinkles and dimples in perfect combination, the smile which told Clive that, wonderfully, everything was going to be fine, at last. 'Yes, Clive, I will. And by all means lose the blazer, but keep the jokes.' Now they were both smiling at each other, with the complete lack of reserve, inhibition, distraction and qualification that only those who love know but the less fortunate can see when loved photographs lover.

'So, everything *is* all right for you,' said the waitress.

JUNE TURNED AWAY FROM THE TEASHOP. SHE'D ONLY BEEN five minutes late, but there was no one there remotely resembling Clive's photograph (she had fancied he bore a bit of a likeness to Cary Grant in *North By Northwest*). It wasn't the first time she'd been stood up; this, though felt particularly bitter and hopeless, on a dank day heading grimly towards a lonely Christmas, with no one to plan a future with over the sherry: the River cruises, the nice meals out, and what to do with the surprising amount of money Ron's untimely death (struck down on the 17th by a rogue ball from the 3rd) had brought to her. But it was more than that; more than the hard dark November cold; more than the fuss, the anticipation, the waste of a good hair-do: no, it was the sight of that pair in the teashop, oblivious to everything including their ordinariness, such was their luminous delight in each other. June walked back to the station, alone, through a Bath that had seen it all before, past the angels, still unmoved.

'In a Bath Teashop'
by John Betjeman

'Let us not speak, for the love we bear one another –
Let us hold hands and look.'
She, such a very ordinary little woman;
He, such a thumping crook;
But both, for a moment, little lower than the angels
In the teashop's ingle-nook.

The background to this, one of Betjeman's most famous – and best – poems is not so romantic. In 1944, he was working at the Admiralty in Bath for a top secret department which produced information bulletins on bomb damage and supplies. His immediate superior was Richard Hughes, author of A High Wind in Jamaica; *his base, rather splendidly, was Major Davis's Empire Hotel. The work was not demanding – Betjeman told Nancy Mitford life was 'wonderfully boring' – and left him time to write and make radio programmes. He was away from his wife, Penelope, and had the opportunity to exercise his famously roving eye. Alice Jennings was the Programme Engineer on a contribution he recorded with his fellow poet, Geoffrey Grigson, for the BBC in Bristol. Alice and Betjeman had a brief, secret affair.*

Betjeman, a wistful but determined conservationist, was for many years a trustee of the Bath Preservation Trust. In 1973, he contributed an introductory poem to The Sack of Bath, *a thundering broadside by* The Times *journalist Adam Fergusson against the bulldozers which were, as he has said, 'still destroying huge stretches of what had been a complete Georgian town – not the grandest bits like the Baths and the Assembly Rooms where the visitors went, or the Crescents where they stayed, but, in their thousands, the little houses of the true 18th-century Bathonians. I am talking of the chair-carriers, the grooms, the buhl-cutters, the porters, the builders, the wig-makers, the shopkeepers; yes, and the pimps, pickpockets and prostitutes – all the people who lived full-time in that contemporary Las Vegas.' The book proved astonishingly influential, largely halting this indiscriminate but often well-intentioned demolition of minor but historic buildings providing frame, scale and context to great cities all around the world, and preventing the prophecy of Betjeman's last two lines:*

> *Goodbye to old Bath. We who loved you are sorry*
> *They've carted you off by developer's lorry.*

After 'In a Bath Teashop' was published, Alice Jennings wrote to Betjeman, 'You may be a thumping crook, but I'm not an ordinary little woman'.

Still, they did write to one another every year until he died.

See:

> *Sally Lunn's Historic Eating House & Museum, 4 North Parade Passage, Bath BA1 1NX (sallylunns.co.uk).*
>
> *Victoria Art Gallery, Bridge Street, Bath, BA2 4AT (victorigal.org.uk). There are fine works by THOMAS GAINSBOROUGH (1727–1788) in the gallery. Gainsborough spent sixteen years in Bath, working his way up to Queen Square by dint of his portraits, charm and sometimes dangerous energy. There are seven of his paintings at the Holburne, including his famous and mighty portrayal of the Byam family. His portrait of Captain William Wade, Beau Nash's rather more elegant successor as Master of Ceremonies, has hung, with*

interruptions, at the Assembly Rooms since Gainsborough presented it. The two prodigies, THOMAS LAWRENCE (1769–1830), and THOMAS BARKER (1769–1847), both come to Bath to make their reputations, and are well represented in the gallery. Barker's self-portrait is a particular delight of ambition and self-confidence.

The Empire Hotel, 4 Grand Parade, Bath BA2 4DF.

Read:

John Betjeman, Collected Poems, *1989, published by Hodder & Stoughton, with whose kind permission* 'In A Bath Teashop' *is reproduced.*
Betjeman, *by AN Wilson, 2006.*
The Sack of Bath, *by Adam Fergusson, 1973.*

At the Christmas Market

DO YOU BELIEVE IN GHOSTS? I USED TO GIVE THE possibility short sympathy, mostly because I believed a large part of a father's job is to appear stolid, dull and down-to-earth, the better to calm potentially dangerous imaginings, the sort of sensible man who used to puff pensively on a pipe, sacrificing sensitivity for the good of the young, puff, puff. My son, though, rather splendidly scuttled this pose by asking me how I could be sure that many of the people we pass on the street and elsewhere are not ghosts.

Well, indeed. A thought to hold tight when you visit the Bath Christmas Market. Have you been? A lot of people. Ranks of wooden chalets mostly selling any amount of gifts your family and friends never knew they needed. Candles, lanterns, 'personalised' pillows, 'personalised' glass Christmas tree baubles, silver reindeers, frosted jewellery and much more, all reflecting off the lights and glass as dusk turns to cold winter dark. And should you be seized with a sudden hunger, there are any number of solutions: sausages and fudge, pancakes and doughnuts and waffles, heavy savoury and sweet scents that crowd the air along with the constant murmur and hum of insistent shoppers who surge and eddy through by the coachload.

As it becomes dark, it's easier to be beguiled by the chalets, which in daytime more resemble rows of little sheds of the type you buy from the garden centre. Now the dark closes around them, softens their outline in the light and shadows. Most are brightly lit within, but some are less so. There used to be a chalet specialising in magic, but it seems to have disappeared. Shoppers are engaged, harassed, beguiled or more intent on sausages. Sellers are bright or not so bright, depending on what kind of day they have had, and how cold it is. Some bid to attract the passers, some just sit, quiet, waiting in various shades of hope.

Now is when, depending on your inclination and imagination, you might fancy that all Bath is with you. This is a scene which has been familiar for at least two thousand years, possibly longer if you believe pigs can fly. This is when my son's thought takes flight, when you cannot be quite sure of the people you pass. That man, for example, the one examining the offers and moving on with the wry smile of one who has been here and done that, looked very much like Clive. The blonde, middle-aged woman selling the shawls and scarves and pashminas could be Alison, or Constance.

The elderly man moving slowly with a stick and throwing loud remarks back over his shoulder to the person of colour who is not listening; the old lady with the faraway look enjoying the street entertainers, her head moving side to side in a jaunty way as her feet tap; the Georgian living statue with ribbons at his knee who just winked; the small north African man impeccably dressed and poised: could they be? I cannot tell you. Some of the entertainers certainly look familiar, especially the bossy one with the squint busy securing audience participation, and the clown juggling and capering. Surely, too, over there, by the stall selling rustic effect photo frames, that's June, the rich widow Clive failed to meet? It is; that's Gerald with her, nice chap, golfer, been looking for someone since Anita died. They've just met; Gerald was coming out of evensong and she had something in her eye (she said).

Over there, a man with a twinkling eye and a goatee of a beard is closely examining a novelty stall, with particular attention to the whoopee cushions, while his wife looks on with an accustomed resigned impatience. But you're getting a little peckish yourself and would like to buy one of those interesting pies the round chap who looks like a cook is selling next door to Alison or Constance, but there's quite a press around his chalet, including an eager small boy with his sister and mother, slightly distracted, and a knot of men of varying heights obviously together and dressed in their Sunday best, very smart. The odd thing is that although the round chap is selling pie after pie, the queue never changes. Next door the ruddy-faced fellow seems to be selling rather more of his buns than his biscuits, but you can't get close to him, either. You give up and move along to the chalet selling CDs run by a slight man with wistfulness in his eyes, playing a jaunty 1930s sort of tune which is almost familiar. His is not such a popular offer, but somehow you cannot attract his attention.

Now the market is running down, people are drifting away, including a kindly looking man with a limp and his friend, who is wearing the sort of hat that only someone who enjoys being looked at would wear: is that a hint of rouge? And that cannot, surely, be Rebecca, abandoning her well for a quick one at The Saracen's Head?

The pie man has gone, and the wistful one. Wary of the shapes you can't quite make out in the shadows, you leave the Abbey Churchyard, passing the Pump Room, noting through the windows that there is a Christmas costume bash; the Bennets are well represented, but cannot compete with the number of Darcys. Over there is a busker, sitting, half-hidden in the shadows, with a pudding-bowl haircut, playing a pleasingly ethereal tune on some sort of stringed instrument. An instinct tells you not to look back up at the Abbey front; you put some hastily gathered coins into his rather attractive bowl; he, or perhaps it is a she, looks up at you with a look that is somehow sad and serene at the same time.

Out then, onto Stall Street, where a large deerhound is watching his master, a man of military bearing with a slight stoop, who is standing with a Roman soldier – possibly one they employ at the Roman baths for effect, although it is a little late for that. The man with the dog is gesturing at Arlington House, where once stood the

Grand Pump Room Hotel. They are joined by another man carrying a roll of architectural drawings under his arm, who shakes his head and points in the direction of Queen Square, the Circus and the Royal Crescent. The military man waves equally vigorously towards the Grand Parade and the Empire Hotel. They walk off, narrowly avoiding a Sedan chair – yes! – hurrying the other way with a tall chairman at the front and a small chairman at the back, grumbling. Inside is a distinguished looking old fellow with silver curls, asleep with a smile, dreaming of the sky. The chair swings round into York Street and the clatter and the cursing fades away.

For a moment, the city is quiet and empty, lost in its past. As does happen, sometimes, in Bath.

General Reading

Books:

A History of Bath, *by Graham Davis and Penny Bonsall, 2006.*

The Royal Crescent Book of Bath, *by James Crathorne, 1998.*

A Traveller's History of Bath, *by Richard and Sheila Tames, 2009.*

A Window on Bath, *by Kirsten Elliott, 1994.*

Bath, *Valley of the Sacred Spring, by Kim Green, 2004.*

Bath Curiosities, *by Michael Raffael, 2006.*

The Bath Book of Days, *by D G Amphlett, 2014.*

Websites:

bathnewseum.com

bath-preservation-trust.org.uk

bathheritagewatchdog.org

buildinghistory.org

bath.heritage.co.uk

visitbath.co.uk

mayorofbath.co.uk

historyofbath.org

Acknowledgements

FIRST, I WANT TO THANK MY DEAR WIFE, LIV, FOR not only putting up with my various obsessions, including Bath, St Helens RFC, once popular music and elderly jokes, but also for reading the manuscript of this book with professional acuity and aplomb, and suggesting many improvements and felicities. But even she cannot work miracles: any mistakes are entirely mine. Then I must record my thanks to and admiration for the many authors and experts on Bath whose hard-won expertise on the page and online I have so happily borrowed. I have tried to acknowledge all my sources: again, any mistakes have nothing to do with them. A confection of historical fact and fiction for humorous purposes must bow to that pioneer of the genre, *No Bed for Bacon*, by Caryl Brahms and SJ Simon, with a doff of the cap to *1066 And All That*, by WC Sellar and RJ Yeatman. I should like, too, to thank Philippa Lewis, Maria Chambers, Sara Sarre of the Blue Pencil Agency, Victoria Hutchings, archivist for C Hoare & Co, and Anne Buchanan, librarian at Bath Record

Office, for their suggestions, encouragement and help at crucial moments. And Bob Bond, a fellow Lancastrian, for his fine map (bobbond@live.co.uk). Rosie Lowe, Philippa Iliffe and Jack Wedgbury at The Book Guild have been models of patience, courtesy and attention. Finally, I must apologise to Bath for my presumption in attempting to convey your charm and magic on a very short acquaintance. And for at first finding you proud and dowdy before I saw your light and recognised the grace with which you bear more than 2,000 years of gawkers, charmers, chancers and change. Bladud would be very proud!